Fatal
Intentions

Fatal Intentions

True Canadian Crime Stories

BARBARA SMITH

HOUNSLOW

Fatal Intentions: True Canadian Crime Stories

Copyright © 1994 by Barbara Smith

Hounslow Press
A member of the Dundurn Group

Publishers: Kirk Howard & Anthony Hawke
Editor: Dennis Mills
Printer: Metrolitho Inc., Quebec

Canadian Cataloguing in Publication Data

Smith, Barbara, 1947-
  Fatal intentions

ISBN 0-88882-167-0

1. Murder - Canada. I. Title.

HV6535.C3S55 1994 364.1'523'0971 C94-931402-1

Publication was assisted by the **Canada Council**, the **Ontario Arts Council**, the **Book Publishing Industry Development Program** of the **Department of Canadian Heritage** and the **Ontario Publishing Centre** of the **Ontario Ministry of Culture, Tourism and Recreation.**

Care has been taken to trace the ownership of copyright material used in this book. The author and publisher welcome any information enabling them to rectify any references or credit in subsequent editions.

Printed and bound in Canada

Hounslow Press	Hounslow Press	Hounslow Press
2181 Queen Street East	73 Lime Walk	1823 Maryland Avenue
Suite 301	Headington, Oxford	P.O. Box 1000
Toronto, Canada	England	Niagara Falls, N.Y.
M4E 1E5	OX3 7AD	U.S.A. 14302-1000

CONTENTS

For

Jim, Joe and Greg

For my grandchildren and their peers — who will need forests as much as books — arrangements have been made to plant a sufficient number of trees to compensate for those used in publishing this volume.

ACKNOWLEDGEMENTS

Grateful acknowledgement is made to the following for permission to reprint previously published material:

Barry Pearson and Marjorie Lamb for lines from *The Boyd Gang*. Peter Martin and Associates, Toronto. Copyright © 1976. All rights reserved.

Gopher Books for lines from *The Robert Cook Murder Case*, by Frank Anderson. Copyright © 1978. All rights reserved.

Prentice-Hall for lines from *The Last Dance, Murder In Canada*, by Neil Boyd. Copyright © 1988. All rights reserved.

The (Montreal) *Gazette* for lines by Fern Larosse and other staff writers. Copyright © 1949, 1950, 1951. All rights reserved.

The *Calgary Herald* for lines by a staff writer. Copyright © 1978. All rights reserved.

The *Winnipeg Free Press* for lines by Brian Cole, Bill Holden, Steve Whysall, and staff writers. Copyright © 1978 and 1979. All rights reserved.

The Canadian Press for lines written by William Stewart, Oscar Tremblay, Richard Daignault, and other writers. Copyright © 1949 and 1950.

PREFACE

The idea for this book grew from one of my previous books, *Deadly Encounters: True Crime Stories of Alberta*. My experience with that project had introduced me to crime stories as a unique and legitimate way to look at an area's social history. I wondered if Canadians, generally, would share my perspective, and so I proposed the idea for this book, somewhat tentatively, to Tony Hawke of Hounslow Press. To my delight, Tony immediately responded with equal doses of enthusiasm and support. The venture was underway.

Much to my surprise, *Fatal Intentions* bears only a little resemblance to the book I initially had in mind. Cases for possible inclusion came and went. Often I'd be on the track of a great story only to have the whole thing fall flat somewhere along the way.

In one instance my family and I decided a story was simply too dangerous for me to take on. After well over ten years, an unsolved murder in the Maritimes is actively being investigated very close to my home on the prairies. We agreed that shedding light on a situation that a murderer has successfully covered up, so far, was best left to the police.

Other Canadian crime stories, which on first examination seemed full of twists and turns, failed to stand up under scrutiny. In these cases what I'd heard was, apparently, based only in rumour and inuendo — terrific stories but certainly not "true crime." This was always disappointing, but at least if I ever decide to write fiction I'll have a large supply of plots on hand!

In making the final selections for *Fatal Intentions*, I tried to choose crimes that were not only interesting in themselves but also representative of either their time or place, or both. The story of Edwin Boyd and his flamboyant fellow bank robbers is a good example. Their exploits shocked and yet fascinated post-World-War-II Torontonians. Inflation and improved security precautions have since combined to reduce bank robbery from a vocation for high rolling criminals to acts of desperation, and rarely worth the risks involved.

Other situations have changed little. In Alberta, the Robert Cook case of 1959 was echoed 32 years later in the Gavin Mandin case. But, was the last hanging in Alberta a fatal error?

And, of course, the passage of years hasn't altered human beings' more base qualities. Greed, jealousy, self-pity, and self-aggrandization continue, as always, to provide motives for crime.

Every attempt has been made to reproduce the stories as accurately as possible. In a few cases, dialogue has been created to clarify situations; however, when it was available I relied on actual accounts. For this reason I am indebted to the painstaking work of many newspaper reporters. Because not all stories in the press carry bylines, some of those reporters must, unfortunately, remain nameless. Others are specified in the endnotes. Whether identified or not, those people have my sincere admiration and thanks.

I would also like to acknowledge the following people:

Barry Pearson turned up one of the few remaining copies of his book, *The Boyd Gang*, which he co-authored nearly twenty years ago with Marjorie Lamb. The authors also sent me a videotape copy of *The Boyd Gang* movie, which they also wrote. Both are treasured collector's items. I thank you for those and, in addition, for generously granting copyright permission.

Jack Webster, historian with the Metropolitan Toronto Police, allowed me to borrow documents from the museum's Boyd Gang collection. These gave me increased insight and a feel for the story that otherwise would have been missing.

Author Frank Anderson of Saskatoon, Saskatchewan, was endlessly generous with research material, valuable advice and copyright permission.

Paul Salter and Andrew Geider of Canadian Airlines kindly supplied the photo of the DC-3.

Jo-Anne Christensen of Edmonton arranged for research material from Jim Harrison, news director of CHNL Radio in Kamloops, British Columbia. I thank you both for your support.

Phyllis Beaulieau and Alan Allnutt of the *Gazette* in Montreal, John Sullivan of the *Winnipeg Free Press*, and Steve Roberts and Tanis Biedler of the *Calgary Herald* all went out of their way to see that my copyright permission requests were handled expeditiously.

Research material for the story "No Fool Like An Old Fool" was purchased from Elizabeth Pacey of Halifax. My thanks, too, to Anne-Marie White of the Halifax *Herald's* library for her assistance.

Even members of my own family were frequently called into service. My younger daughter, Robyn, did a tremendous amount of early research for me and then, as deadline approached, made several trips to the British Columbia Provincial Archives in order to read and copy archival newspapers. My older daughter, Debbie, read many first drafts and patiently listened to concerns that I was always sure were earth-shattering in magnitude. And most importantly, my husband, Bob, not only offered constant support but also took over specific aspects of information gathering and sorting, thus leaving me free to concentrate on writing. Thank you.

There are two people, however, who have really made this book possible. Without them, no matter how hard I worked or how much co-operation I received from others my idea could not have become a book. Tony Hawke of Hounslow Press: I have come to count on your positive outlook as an indispensible fringe benefit of my career. And Dennis Mills: I thank you for enhancing my work with your deft editing skills.

SIEGE AT OAK LAKE

On Monday, January 23, 1978, Canadian newspapers informed their readers of Paolo Violi's murder. They described him as an "underworld kingpin."[1] While the news of any death offends the mortal core in all of us, there really wasn't much in Violi's life with which the average Canadian could identify.

The man "allegedly controlled organized crime in Montreal [from] the bar next door to Violi's ice-cream parlor ... [and] went down in a hail of bullets after two hooded men burst into the poolroom bar."[2]

Such news seems slightly exotic to ordinary, law-abiding citizens who get up and go to work each day in order to make a living.

That same day, however, newspapers in Calgary reported two other murders as well. One was the strangulation death of a local businessman. Police withheld the man's name but revealed he'd been found nude in his southwest Calgary office.

Every daily newspaper in the country carried reports of the third killing. While on a routine stolen vehicle investigation in the small Manitoba town of Virden, three Mounties had been shot, one killed.

The shooting marked the beginning of five days of a horribly memorable time for all those involved.

On the evening of Sunday, January 22, 1978, all appeared normal at the Countryside Inn Motel near the Trans-Canada Highway in Virden. The wind made the minus zero temperatures feel even colder than it was. Several travelers, including a couple registering as Mr. and Mrs. Maurice Crystal, of Surrey, B.C., checked into the motel. The couple said they were headed east, and they used a credit card to pay for their night's lodging.

The procedure resembled that of hundreds of guests who had stayed at the Inn. Travelers on Canada's main east/west thoroughfare, using credit cards, provided the Countryside Inn with its bread and butter. The only difference between the Crystals' registration and those of previous lodgers was the bulky bandage on Mr. Crystal's right hand. It made writing difficult; so the signature on the registration form didn't bear much resemblance to that on the credit card.

Once Sandy Bohonis, the motel owner, had handed the room key to the Crystals, he didn't give the couple another thought. When Sandy and his wife closed the office and switched off the Vacancy sign for the night, there was no indication anything was amiss. They had no way of knowing that a truck-rental firm in Vancouver had finally given up waiting for "Donald A." Archer of Surrey to return the white, one-ton van now parked outside Room 20 of their motel.

When the forty-two-year-old Archer had signed the contract to lease the late-model vehicle, he said he needed to keep it for two days. It was now a month overdue and reported stolen.

While on their nightly patrol, RCMP in Virden noted the similarity between a truck parked outside the Countryside Inn and one described in a nation-wide report of stolen vehicles. The truck-rental company records indicated a man named Donald A. Archer had leased the van some weeks before. Police records listed outstanding warrants for a man meeting Archer's description and known to use a string of aliases, including the one on the rental company's form. Police records also showed outstanding warrants for Archer's wife, Dorothy.

Four officers in three police cruisers arrived at the Countryside Inn to investigate. Corporal Russell Hornseth, the highest ranking of the officers responding, went ahead of Constables John O'Ray, Dennis Onofrey and Candace Smith. Hornseth knocked on the door and called out to the occupants, identifying himself as a police officer.

The door marked "20" opened a crack. A disheveled-looking, middle-aged man poked his head around the door. He barked an order into the dimly lit room.

"Hide behind the shower door," Archer ordered the woman.

Possibly uncomfortable with the flurry of activity, Constable Dennis Onofrey drew his gun. Archer saw the flash of metal aimed at his beloved Dorothy. Seconds later, on that winter's night, Onofrey lay dead in the snow just outside the motel.

Archer fired again, hitting Constable Smith, who had run to Onofrey's aid. Hornseth, a few feet behind his fallen colleagues, returned the gunman's fire wounding the woman in the abdomen. Archer's next shot hit Hornseth in the head.

Constable O'Ray had gone to the back of the motel in case the suspects had tried to escape through a window. The Archers weren't aware of his presence and thought all the police intent on arresting them were now unconscious.

"We've gotta get outa here. Can you make it?" Archer asked the injured woman.

She nodded and the two ran out into the parking lot. "The van's almost out of gas. If the keys are in the cruiser we'll use it instead," the man said.

Constable O'Ray emerged from his post in the rear of the building in time to see the red tail lights of the stolen cruiser recede from view. He ran to his downed colleagues before radioing for help. Sobbing, he advised his dispatcher, "Dennis is dead. Candace and Russell look bad too."

Twenty-eight-year-old Dorothy Archer moaned in pain as her accomplice-husband drove the stolen RCMP cruiser away from the scene of the shooting.

"I'll get some help," the man assured his injured partner. "We'll get you patched up and we'll be outa here. They'll never get us."

Archer didn't feel as confident as he sounded; he had no arsenal of guns and ammunition. He also knew they wouldn't get far in a stolen police cruiser. They'd need to make a few adjustments to their armory and mode of transportation.

"You gotta get me fixed. I'll never make it like this. There's a big hunk of lead in me,"[3] the woman responded in a strained voice.

They'd only gotten a few miles from Virden when Archer noticed a farmhouse in the village of Routledge, not far off the road. He knew he couldn't risk going much farther, and he speculated, quite accurately, that there wouldn't be another town for a while.

"We'll stop in there and get what we need." Archer said. "I'll make them take us to the nearest doctor. Once he's got the bullet out of you, we'll get outa Canada. They'll never get us. We'll be safe, you'll see. We'll get a little place somewhere in Europe or the States. I'll get a job and we'll leave all of this behind us."

With visions of white picket fences dancing in their combined heads, the two turned into farmer Dave Penny's driveway. The family's dogs barked madly at the intruders, waking up the man, his wife, two daughters, and an overnight guest. As Penny opened the front door to check on the dogs, the two intruders pushed their way inside.

"We need more guns and ammunition, and my wife needs a doctor," Archer instructed, brandishing a rifle in one hand and a revolver in the other.

The startled farmer replied: "No one here has any medical training, and we don't keep firearms in the house. I can take you to a doctor in Oak Lake but that's the best I can do."

"Where can I get guns? I need more guns or no one will cooperate with me," the gunman demanded, waving his pistol menacingly.

"Please don't hurt anyone. We'll do what you want but just don't hurt anyone."

Penny's wife joined him in the front hall but only momentarily. She left to tend to their younger daughter who'd been wakened by the commotion and was crying out in fright.

"All right," Archer growled with a hint of satisfaction in his voice. These people were as scared as he needed them to be. "Get everyone who's here in living room. I'll take one of your kids and your wife with me for help. We've already killed some cops so you'd better believe we're not afraid to use these things."

"No. Leave my wife and daughters," David Penny bargained. "Take me instead. I know the neighbours better than they do anyway."

Archer looked confused for a moment but then turned to his injured wife.

"I'll tie them up and rip out the phones. You can stay here to watch them. Don't untie them for anything and don't be afraid to use the gun if you have to, dear."

"I won't, dearie."[4] The coy terms of affection were in sickening contrast to the situation.

Heading the cruiser east once again, Archer used his right hand to steer, and his left to aim his gun at his hostage.

"Go in here," Penny instructed his captor when they reached Lloyd Hatch's farm.

Although it was nearly two o'clock in the morning, Penny knew Lloyd never locked his home. With Archer's gun pressed uncomfortably in his upper back, David Penny led the way up the stairs to the Hatchs' bedroom.

"There's been an accident," Archer offered as an explanation to the sleeping home-owners. "I need guns, ammunition and a car. I've killed now and it doesn't make any difference ... [I'll kill] four or six people if I have to."[5]

Despite having been wakened from a deep sleep, Lloyd Hatch immediately assessed the seriousness of the situation.

Wilma Hatch later recalled that although she knew the man "meant business ... the only time I was afraid was when they went to tie up my husband because I knew that look in his eyes. He didn't want to be tied up."[6]

They realized, though, they had no alternative: not only was he armed, but he was so wound up and tense that the couple "wondered if he was high on drugs" because "he never stopped talking." [7]

During his non-stop babble, Archer explained, among other things, his extreme dislike of the police, most particularly the RCMP. When Wilma Hatch heard that, she thanked whatever power had watched out for her earlier that day. While cleaning the house she had moved a large, leafy plant from one spot to another. She intended the move only to increase the amount of sunlight the plant received. The woman knew she wouldn't leave it there for more than a day or two because it blocked a picture on the wall — a picture she and Lloyd were understandably proud of — a photograph of their youngest son, Fred, in full RCMP dress. [8]

Fortunately, Archer's interest in the Hatchs' home didn't extend to its decor. His only interest lay in getting Lloyd Hatch's guns and ammunition and then getting away from the man's house as quickly as possible.

"You drive," he instructed Penny, handing him the keys to the cruiser.

Archer's chatter showed no signs of abating. It wore on Dave Penny's already taut nerves.

"If this doctor [in Oak Lake] can't fix my wife up, there's no point in me living any longer." Archer told his hostage, "She's my life. I'm just a guy who's done a few things wrong and now it's all starting to catch up to me."[9]

That revelation offered no reassurance to Penny. He declined comment and chose, instead, to concentrate on driving the cruiser back to his home. He had no trust in the stability of either his captor or the woman guarding his family, and he'd only be relieved when he saw his wife and children were all right.

As Penny opened his front door, he relaxed slightly. The group in the living room sat exactly as they had when he and Archer had left to get the guns.

"Come on, dear," Archer called to his wife. "We've got the guns now. This man'll take us to the doctor and then we'll be out of here."

Without daring to speak to his wife or children, David Penny once again got into the police car. He headed east to the town of Oak Lake, Manitoba. At last count, its population registered 340, but only one citizen was really important to David Penny at the moment.

Born in Poland and educated in Belgium, the sixty-four-year-old Markus Scherz had served the town of Oak Lake for the past twenty-five years. He and his wife, Stephanie, had raised their children there. The couple were well known and well liked members of the community. Penny knew that even under these trying circumstances Scherz would keep his head and not make the situation any worse.

This was no small consolation to Penny because he expected it wouldn't be long before the police caught up with Archer.

Being the only doctor for miles around meant Markus Scherz was often disturbed through the night. So he didn't even register much surprise when he opened his front door to the injured Mrs. Archer, her husband, and their unwilling escort.

"My wife's been shot," Archer told the doctor as he guided his wife into the house.

"We're in some trouble here, as well," Penny added, indicating the guns his captors carried.

The doctor sighed audibly, turned to his wife and said calmly, "Stephanie, we'll need to see to this woman's injuries right away."

Drawing her housecoat around her, Mrs. Scherz led the patient into her husband's examining room. Markus Scherz knew with only a cursory examination that there was little he could do for her in his office.

"This injury requires more care than I can give your wife here," he began. "She'll need to go to the hospital. I'd recommend you not waste any time getting her there."

"Will she die?" Archer asked.

"I can't say anything for sure, but her chances are much better if she's in a hospital. She needs surgery. Take her to Brandon. It's just east of here. It's close. It wouldn't take you even an hour to get her there."

Drops of perspiration stood out on Archer's forehead. He looked at Dorothy huddling in pain on the examining table.

"My life is nothing without her, but I can't risk the trip to Brandon. The place could be crawling with cops by now. We'd never make it to the hospital. Once they find out we've shot up some cops they'll bring us down anyway they can. No. I can't risk taking her to Brandon," Archer concluded.

He remained silent for a moment as he thought through the situation.

"Phone for an ambulance. Have them take her to Brandon to the hospital. I'll hold you three here with me until I know she's well enough to keep travelling with me." Again Archer paused, "Yes, that's what to do. Call for the ambulance and hurry! Can't you see my wife's in pain?"

The doctor certainly could see the woman's pain. He could also see that this strange assortment of people crowded into his examining room was in grave danger. The perpetrator was armed; he'd already shot, if not killed, more than one police officer, and he was becoming irrational. Dr. Scherz picked up the phone and requested an ambulance. He ignored the dispatcher's request for details and only advised both extreme haste and caution.

Relieved that his wife would soon be receiving the care she needed, Archer turned his thoughts inward. Dorothy might be in the hospital for several days. How could he guard three people for those many hours? He'd need to sleep at some point. If that cop hadn't shot Dorothy, none of this would have happened, his distressed mind reasoned illogically. If she'd been able to stay with him, they could have taken turns sleeping, secure in the knowledge the other one stood guard.

He glanced again at his wife. The injection the doctor had given her to ease the pain must have begun to take effect. She lay quietly on the table listening as the older woman spoke soothingly to her. By the time the ambulance arrived she was barely conscious, unable to offer Archer any words of encouragement.

He'd carry on without her for now.

"Would you like something hot to drink?"

"Huh?" Archer replied uncomprehendingly.

"Would you like a cup of tea or coffee? Oh, and by the way, I don't know your name. Mine is Stephanie," the doctor's wife offered.

"Cliff, just call me Cliff, okay?"

"Yes, Cliff. That'll be fine. You mustn't worry about your wife anymore. She'll be fine. Would you like something to eat or drink?"

The last things Archer expected from his captors were kindness and hospitality, but with the daylight hours of Monday, January 23, 1978, still several hours away, the strange little group sat down for a light meal.

"Turn on the radio, would you?" Archer requested. "They'll be on to me now. I want to know what's happening out there."

The next news broadcast informed the four holed up in the doctor's home-cum-office on Railway Street in Oak Lake that the police were most assuredly "on to" Archer. They had cordoned off the area surrounding the Scherzes' house, and a sharp-shooter lay in waiting out there somewhere. Television and radio stations repeated the news until noon the following day. For most residents of southern Manitoba it was the first indication that one of their normally quiet neighbourhoods had been the scene of a terrible tragedy.

Archer welcomed Stephanie's offer of food. But after eating he felt sleepy, and the important matter of wakefulness came to his mind again.

"Doc," he called to the man across the room. "What can you give me to keep me awake? You guys have got stuff like that. Stuff to keep a person awake. I know you do so don't try bluffing. I'll need something that'll keep me going for a couple of days at least."

"I do have some amphetamines but they won't keep you awake for days. Nothing I know of will."

"Give me some of them now, and when I get tired I'll take some more. Have you got lots?"

"Enough," Markus Scherz hedged. "Enough to suit your purpose."

"Give them to me and then show me where your phone is. I need to get things underway here. This waiting around is making me agitated," Archer complained.

"I'd like to get some sleep now, if I could," David Penny said quietly.

"You're not going upstairs," Archer warned gruffly.

"You're welcome to rest on our chesterfield if you think you'd be comfortable there," Stephanie Scherz offered. "I'll get you a blanket."

"And I have some paperwork I should attend to if it's all right with you," Markus Scherz said. "If we're all going to be here for awhile, it's foolish to waste the time."

"What am I going to do?" the gunman asked in the tone of a spoiled child who's no longer the centre of attention.

"We can chat, if you like," Scherz's wife suggested.

As Archer nodded his assent the telephone rang. For a second no one moved.

"Get it!" Archer ordered, jumping to his feet at the second ring and waving his gun first in the direction of the doctor and then the phone.

"Hello," Markus Scherz said into the receiver, wondering briefly about that trait that causes humans to revert to normal behaviour in such abnormal circumstances.

"It's the police here. Do you have an intruder there, Dr. Scherz?"

"Yes, yes sir, that's right, we do."

"Has anyone been injured?"

"No, we're all right here." Markus started to explain that they were being treated well when the gunman became anxious and grabbed the phone from him.

"How's my wife?" Archer barked into the receiver.

"We've checked on your wife and she's resting comfortably. A full recovery's expected."

"Good. She'd better. You people better make sure she's all right or you'll be sorry. A cop shot her, you know. It's all his fault. He shouldn't have pointed his gun at my wife. That's the only reason I fired on them. Are they all right? I didn't kill anyone did I?"

The officer at the other end of the phone line took a breath.

"Yes, I'm sorry, you did. One of our officers is dead and two others are in the hospital. One in serious condition."

The horror and enormity of the situation finally registered with the cop-killer who wanted to be called "Cliff."

"Oh, my god," he said, fighting to control his voice.

"Yes, Constable Dennis Onofrey died at the scene."

"I can't talk anymore now," Archer announced between sobs. "My god, I can't talk."

The heavy black receiver fell from his hand. For a moment Markus Scherz wondered if Cliff might drop the gun as well. If he did, would anyone have a chance to safely snatch it away?

The doctor picked up the dangling telephone and spoke into it.

"Look, whatever you've told him has upset him. We're sitting ducks here. Please keep that in mind. How's the man's wife? I sent her to the hospital earlier this morning."

After a pause the doctor spoke again, "Good. Good. Yes, I'll tell him. Wait. I think Cliff may want to talk to you again himself."

Offering the gunman the phone, the doctor explained: "They say your wife's doing well and that the hospital will release her in a couple of days. Do you want to say anything more to the police?"

Archer regained his composure by the time he took the phone.

"I want you to patch my wife up and bring her to me here. And when you do, you can also bring me $50,000 in cash, no wait, make that $100,000 and an airplane to get the hell out of Canada to somewhere safe. I'll also need a letter from Prime Minister Trudeau stating that authorities won't try to bring [us] back if [we] are accepted by another country." [10]

"We'll see what we can do for you, sir." The officer on the other end of the phone knew from his training not to commit himself or anyone else to anything in these sorts of situations. "Do you still have David Penny there?"

"Yes, and he's fine. He's asleep right now in the living room."

"Okay, Cliff. Can you let me speak to the doctor or his wife again, please?"

"Not for long," the gunman replied, hoping to remind these people who was in charge here. He, and only he, would call the shots. He'd been pushed around enough. Now he had hostages, guns, and control. And no one had better forget it.

"Hello," the doctor said again as Archer handed him the phone. "Thank you for your concern, but I'm sure we'll do fine here. Cliff seems quite concerned for our well being as, I must tell you, we are for his."

Oh great, thought the experienced officer at the other end of the phone line. The Stockholm Syndrome[11] at work again and it's starting after just a few hours. He'd seen this phenomenon before and it made these cases difficult to handle. Apparently some very human part of a hostage's psyche can begin to side with the captor.

"We're at work here to determine who this man is and how best to deal with the situation. Please don't worry. No one's going to storm your house. Your safety and that of your wife and David Penny are our prime concerns. We'll be staying in constant telephone contact. Hanging up the phone won't break the connection. Just lift the receiver if you need us and tell the others that as well, if you would please."

"Yes, I'll let Cliff know what the arrangements are, but for now I don't think anything more can be accomplished by this conversation and I'd like to get back to my paperwork if you don't mind," the doctor said, replacing the handset in its cradle.

"All we can do now is wait," Stephanie Scherz advised no one in particular. "It could take days."

As the stand-off in Oak Lake continued, police reinforcements and the media converged on the town. Few businesses and no schools opened

Monday, and residents remained in their homes. Some of the closest neighbours were instructed by the police to find safer, temporary accomodations. Agnes McQuarrie, who lived just behind the Scherzes, was escorted from her cottage so quickly that she forgot her teeth. The police wouldn't let her return to get them.

Another neighbour, eighty-one-year-old Mrs. Doherty, spoke to the press on the phone. She explained that "she was keeping her doors locked, lights out and drapes closed." She anticipated spending the day listening for reports on the "radio and trying to keep busy." The woman's sense of humour obviously wasn't affected by the nearby threat because she added, "I don't know whether I've got enough sense to get upset."[12]

Families of the injured police officers made their way to the Brandon General Hospital, and Monsignor R.J.H. Larabee prepared to officiate at the funeral of a young man he had baptized only twenty-seven years earlier.

In Calgary, the family of Maurice Crystal also made funeral preparations. His sixteen-year-old son had found his father's nude body on Sunday evening in his real-estate office in southwest Calgary. He had been strangled. The motive wasn't immediately apparent; however, as the Archers had used his credit card to rent their motel room, it might merely have been robbery.

Inside the doctor's house and in its immediate vicinity, there was little activity. Mounties set up road blocks at all the highway entrances to the town. Snipers lay poised around the Scherzes' house, and a police van containing state-of-the-art surveillance equipment stood nearby. Life as the Oak Lake community had known it ceased completely. Police reinforcements arrived throughout the day. They tried to make themselves as comfortable as possible while taking turns working twelve-hour shifts and sleeping in the Oak Lake school gymnasium. The media rivalled the police in numbers. The Oakland Hotel experienced a surge of business such as the manager Cy Kerr had never seen before. And the hotel's beer parlour became a centre for a litany of speculations and rumours. By sundown Monday the town's population had, temporarily, increased by more than one hundred.

Something of a pattern developed in the Scherzes' home. The trust that grew between the hostages and their warden proved sufficient to allow the three captives to roam about the house.

At press time the next day, there had been no change in the situation, so the headline in the *Winnipeg Free Press* offered the following information: "Town remains in state of siege."[13]

In the Scherzes' home, the hostages struggled to control their stress-induced mood swings. They ate and slept in as regular as routine as possible. Townsfolk who knew the doctor's family assured police that Stephanie Scherz always kept her kitchen well stocked. This provided the classic "good news/bad news" scenario: a shortage of food might force an end to the siege, but it might also mean additional dangers for anyone delivering supplies.

While the tension in the house was not as acute as it had been at first, there were moments of increased concern, and no clear-cut avenues of escape. Despite his regular use of amphetamines, Archer dozed off several times. He kept his gun in his hand while he napped, and jolted into consciousness at the least sound. When Archer went to the bathroom he always took one of the hostages with him.

"Anyone tries to escape and I'll kill whoever's left," he warned. Archer's tone and behaviour gave his prisoners every reason to believe he intended to keep his word.

By daybreak on Tuesday, January 24, hostages and captor knew one another well. David Penny gained strength by telling Archer of his own deep and abiding Christian beliefs. The Scherzes may or may not have shared Penny's religious convictions, but the couple's natural warmth contributed to the precariously peaceful atmosphere. If Markus Scherz had been a less caring person, he would never have practiced medicine in a small town. As his wife and helpmate for many years, Stephanie Scherz, evidently both admired and reflected those qualities.

The personalities of the hostages and the tense situation created fertile soil for the Stockholm Syndrome to flourish. And flourish it did. The police maintained constant telephone communication with the four. Every hour they rang the phone and requested an update on the state of affairs. Stephanie Scherz responded to one call with a curt plea to "leave us alone."[14]

The only information the hostages had of Archer came from the man himself. He managed to paint a sympathetic self-portrait by forgetting to mention a number of important issues. In reality their abductor had never made much of an effort to earn an honest living. To assist him in his law-breaking career, "Cliff" adopted a number of aliases, including Cliff Gorril, Clifford Ray Gorril, Donald Archer and Donald Alfred Archer.

Vancouver-area police departments showed outstanding warrants for several of those names and a man meeting Archer's description. These warrants specified a variety of offenses, including fraud, jumping bail, and false pretenses. He chose to keep another incident in his recent past from his kidnap victims — the cold-blooded murder of a Calgary businessman.

Both the RCMP and the Calgary police suspected the Archers had murdered Maurice Crystal on their way through to Manitoba. In an attempt to contain the potentially volatile hostage-taking, the police withheld the information. Despite this security it didn't take long for reporters to connect the two events. Calgary's police chief, Brian Sawyer, called a press conference on Wednesday, January 25.

"It would be very unwise at this stage [before the Manitoba situation is resolved] to allow the hostage-taker to be made aware of what the police suspect in connection with the homicide here. What's at stake, and I don't want to be overdramatic [sic], is the lives of three people. If any of you disagree, then candidly, it's on your heads if anything goes wrong," Sawyer warned reporters after acknowledging their "enterprising journalistic legwork." [15]

And so everyone involved cooperated as fully as possible. Perhaps this lack of reference to the Alberta killing led Archer to believe either the murder hadn't been discovered or, if it had, no one connected it with him. Whichever scenario he wanted to believe, it fed his self-promotion as "just a guy who got a little out of line, and the roof fell in on me. I just happened to do a couple of things wrong." [16]

He went on to enumerate to his hostages the things he considered he'd done wrong prior to the shootout in Virden. He explained that he "had jumped bail in British Columbia, where he had been arrested for writing bad cheques, and rented a truck which he failed to return."[17] Archer's selective memory neglected to include a history of petty crime, skipping bail, avoiding arrest and, of course, Maurice Crystal's cold, naked body.

But Archer's devotion to his wife was nearly obsessive. By Tuesday night his mood had sunk into depression. He decided the delay of a medical report on his wife's condition meant she'd already died.

Sitting on the living room floor, a dejected Archer ranted, barely coherently, while waving his gun in the air. "I know now my wife's dead. There's nothing left for me to live for if she is dead. We promised each other if she dies I will die."[18]

Only moments later the phone rang. The surgeon at Brandon General Hospital wanted to report the successful completion of Dorothy Archer's surgery. Jubilation quickly replaced depression.

"Oh, my God, my wife is alive. Now I have a reason to live. My wife is alive." [19] The relieved group knelt to offer a prayer of thanks.

Police felt somewhat re-assured by consistent reports from those who knew the Scherzes. All of Oak Lake's residents considered both husband and wife to be pillars of the community. None expressed any concern that the couple would try any foolish heroics. The only worry ever expressed was in reference to Dr. Scherz's heart condition.

Bert Fuller, a neighbour, told reporters, "He's got a bad heart ... he [could] crack under the strain."[20]

That fear may have prompted Markus Scherz's release just before midnight on Wednesday, January 25. Police picked him up from his house and drove him in an unmarked van directly to Brandon General Hospital. Two hours later authorities reported the man in "good condition."[21] What the media didn't know was that Markus Scherz was also a Nazi concentration camp survivor.

Early the next morning Dennis Onofrey's widow and eight hundred others made final preparations for the slain man's funeral. Six of the officer's former colleagues, in full scarlet dress, carried the coffin into St. Mary's Cathedral in Virden. Police from numerous Canadian police forces including the RCMP attended the service.

Manitoba's Premier Sterling Lyon also paid his respects: "I merely want to say what is in the hearts and minds of most Manitobans and to express deep sympathy to Mrs. Onofrey and the family on the loss of her husband ... and to wish godspeed for the recovery of Constable Candace Smith and [Corporal] Russ Hornseth."22

Inside and outside the Scherz home the waiting game continued. By the time the pallbearers lifted Dennis Onofrey's coffin from the hearse for its final journey to the grave, Stephanie Scherz, David Penny, and "Cliff" had fallen into a tedious routine born of eighty hours' captivity.

In areas of Oak Lake furthest away from the doctor's house, day-to-day life slowly resumed. Students, forbidden entry to their school by dozens of RCMP, temporarily attended classes in Virden. Oak Lake's largest restaurant remained closed except to police and reporters. Economic necessity re-opened the town's bank.

Archer's determination began to weaken noticeably. The hostages' sympathy for the man may have fed his fantasies about great amounts of money, safe passage, and asylum in a foreign country. These delusions seemed less and less likely as the hours ticked away. The authorities were considerably better equipped to play the waiting game than Archer was. Even the hostages were more comfortable than Archer. They slept peacefully for several hours at a time whereas Archer continued to depend on catnaps and amphetamines.

Late in the evening of Thursday, January 26, a change in attitude came over Archer.

"What do you think my wife and I'll get if I surrender?" he inquired of his hostages at one point.

"That's hard to say," Penny replied.

"Do you think they'd give me a chance to clear my wife's name? She's getting blamed for something she didn't do. They're blaming her along with me for shooting the Mounties and she didn't fire. Not even once. Dorothy would never shoot anyone."

"If you released us you could ask for an opportunity to pass that message to the press," Penny prompted. "I think you've got a much better chance of getting your way with that idea than the $100,000 and the aircraft you wanted."

"What else should I ask for if I did surrender?" Archer probed.

"Fair treatment," Stephanie Scherz interjected. "Remind the police that you let Markus go and that you've been kind and considerate to us. That should help lighten your sentence."

"I'll go to jail, won't I?"

"No doubt, but if you don't surrender they're going to barge in here eventually, you know that. If that happens we could all be killed, and even if you live through it you'll be given a much longer jail term, I'm sure," Penny reasoned.

"If you give up now, you and your wife can serve your time, and then when you're released you'll still be young enough to get on with your lives," Penny concluded.

All three were very aware of the time. The police's regular hourly call would come any minute now. The two remaining hostages sat in silent tension while Archer's drug-muddled and sleep-deprived mind sorted through his options.

Only the ringing phone broke the tense silence. Neither David Penny nor Stephanie Scherz made any attempt to move toward the phone. There was little left for them to do. The negotiations, if there were to be any, would have to be between Archer and the authorities.

"I don't want to talk right now," Archer growled into the receiver.

Apparently the police were content, for the moment, to take that as sufficient information for this phone call. They knew from experience and training that the situation would likely change, either for better or for worse, within a few hours. The intensity required to maintain a hostage-taking situation just couldn't be spread over many more hours. The human nervous system wears down and then eventually gives out. The police felt encouraged by Archer's display of impatience. It meant a move toward resolution. While they wanted to promote progress by cooperating, they also needed to know that Penny and Mrs. Scherz were still all right.

"Let me talk to Stephanie," the officer requested.

Archer stood silently holding the black receiver out to the doctor's wife. After quickly reassuring the police that both she and Penny remained in good health, she spoke a quick "yes" into the phone and then hung up. Archer had no way of knowing that the word was an affirmative response to the RCMP's suspicions that change was imminent.

The court appointed a Winnipeg lawyer, Hersch Wolch, to represent Archer. The two had spoken briefly over the last few days. With this latest development, the police placed a call to him in the Oakland Hotel. They hoped that Wolch's skills as a defence attorney would soon be required.

At 11 p.m. the police called again.

"We're not ready yet," Penny replied to an unasked question, thereby confirming that the end was near. "Cliff will pick up the phone when he's got this sorted out in his mind. Don't call back. We're all fine in here."

Fully two and a half tension-filled hours later, a nearly incoherent "Cliff" picked the telephone receiver from its cradle. At the other end of the line an officer wearing a headset jolted mentally to attention.

"Let me talk to Wolch," Archer demanded.

Grateful for the foresight his experience had given him, the officer calmly removed his headset and handed it to the lawyer. Everyone at the command post knew the demands would not be nearly as extravagant now, after over ninety hours of self-imposed captivity, as they were when the incident began. With the exception of one specification, both the lawyer and the police officers could have predicted the man's final demands.

Archer uttered that unexpected demand first. He wanted fraud and assault charges against him in both Ontario and British Columbia dropped. After that, the man who shot three Mounties, murdering one, blinding another in the eye and rendering the third infertile, requested a full and competent defence, an hour's visit with his wife, and assurance that he wouldn't be harmed as he gave himself up.

This arranged, Archer offered himself to the authorities with more of a plea than a command.

"Come and get me," he said.

Just after three in the morning, Archer and the two hostages walked out the front door of the Scherzes' house. An unmarked van waited at the end of the driveway. For a few seconds all the players stood still on the snow-covered lawn. This was the moment they'd anxiously awaited. The reality seemed an anticlimax.

Once they descended the front steps, the three gazed out at the battalions of police poised for action.

"Archer," a voice called out through the darkness. "Walk slowly toward us with your hands up. Do what we say and you won't be hurt."

Archer knew what came next. He'd been arrested many times before. He turned to the hostages. For a minute, concern spread that he'd take them back into the house. Instead, he merely embraced the two people. They returned his display of affection and all three walked toward the police with their hands raised and tears streaming down their faces.

The captives and their kidnapper didn't have exclusive rights to emotional overload. Jubilant that the situation had ended without further injuries or loss of life, the RCMP also showed the relief they felt.

"'I love you!' one officer shouted as he hugged another officer." [23]

Police held the press away from the immediate scene, but they were at least able to report a "tired and worn down" Archer gave himself up to "two burly plainclothes officers" [24] who whisked him away to the hospital in Brandon. Here Archer spent the time he'd been promised with his wife and then, under guard, slept for most of Friday.

The two hostages, badly shaken from their ordeal, went to a closer hospital — ironically the hospital in Virden, the town where all the horror began. Doctors examined them both and noted that although the two showed signs of exhaustion their health and spirits remained good.

Less than two hours later, RCMP escorted the Penny family to an unnamed friend's home, and Dr. and Mrs. Scherz were taken to another undisclosed location. The families asked that the press give them a day to recover from their ordeal and arranged to be at the Oak Lake town hall for an official press conference the following evening (Saturday) at six o'clock.

On that Saturday morning, police charged Herbert Bruce Archer, 42, of Surrey, B.C., and Dorothy Lillian Malette, alias Dorothy Archer, 28, also of Surrey, jointly with the murder of Constable Dennis Anthony Onofrey. "Other charges are pending, an RCMP spokesman said." [25] And a court hearing was scheduled for the morning of Monday, January 30, 1978, in Brandon, Manitoba.

Oak Lake life began return to normal. While most people felt grateful that all the excitement had ended, at least one man found the incident provided relief from the usual monotony of his life.

"Bert Fuller, 77, whose house was used by RCMP throughout the siege, was alone again last night. 'I've been alone for three years ever since my wife died,' he said. 'Then this happened and the next thing I know my house is swarming with Mounties. I told them, 'Give me a bullet-proof jacket and I'll go and sort him out myself.' They told me to sit back and relax.'" [26]

A few members of the media stayed behind to cover the Saturday evening press conference, but most of them spent Friday filing final reports and packing up to return home. The dozens of RCMP specialists and constables called in as back-up now prepared to vacate the school that had been their home-away-from-home for the past week.

Their injured colleagues, Constable Smith and Corporal Hornseth, remained in the Brandon General Hospital. They were recuperating and resting as comfortably as could be expected. Although neither of the bullet wounds was life-threatening, they both had long roads to complete recovery. In addition to the physical healing necessary, both would have to come to grips with some profound changes: Candace Smith would never be able to have children, and Russell Hornseth was blind in one eye.

Members of the media remaining to cover the Saturday evening press conference had their suitcases packed and in their cars outside the town hall. They presumed, correctly, that within a couple of hours there would be little news from Oak Lake, Manitoba. They did, however, look forward to an opportunity to question the hostages first-hand. With careful probing, they knew they could collect the intimate details necessary to produce emotion-laden copy. All the reporters entered the town hall planning poignant, full-length features. No one was disappointed.

Touching photo opportunities abounded. Irene Penny comforted her husband, David, as he struggled to maintain his composure while speaking of his three days in captivity and the break-in that had led up to the event.

"'I heard banging on the door and the dogs barking,' Penny said. 'I got up, put on my pants and went out and met him .... He had a rifle in one hand and a revolver in the other. He said, 'Stand right where you are and you won't get hurt.' My daughter was lying on the chesterfield and she woke and was screaming.'" 27

However, David Penny felt, "The worst moment for me was when he told me he was going to take my wife and little girl. I pleaded with him to take me instead and he ... agreed. He said 'if you do what I tell you nothing is going to happen to your wife and family and I believed him and I did everything I possibly could to get him away from my family. After we were about a mile away from my place I relaxed. I thought, well, if I go now at least my family's okay."28

Penny recalled how, while being held at the Scherzes' house he occasionally thought of trying to overpower Archer but decided against it. "I knew it was no good. He slept on the bed and if we so much as moved a muscle his hands were on the gun and his eyes were open. I didn't think I could shoot him even if I did get a gun." 29

Dr. Scherz reported that being the only doctor in a small town, "It was not the first time someone had come at two or three o'clock and had knocked on the door. He [Archer] said, 'Doctor, I have an injured woman I'd like to have you look at.' I said, 'If she's badly hurt you had better bring her into my office.'"30

As soon as he examined Dorothy Archer, Scherz realized he faced more than an ordinary problem. "I said, 'What is going on?'" 31

Archer had briefly explained the shoot-out in Virden and then had begun to tape the doctor's hands together.

"What are you doing? I am a doctor. You want me to look after your wife or don't you want me to look after her?" 32

Scherz also described the terror they felt Tuesday night as Archer waited for news about his wife's health.

"[He] sat on the chesterfield, shaking and perspiring, and then began to motion with the gun. 'We didn't know if he was going to kill himself or all of us,' Dr. Markus Scherz recalled. 'That was the most frightening moment. We will never forget it. You must remember this woman was the Alpha and Omega of his life. He said, 'When she is dead I'll kill myself. If that woman had died we would have all died.'"33

Eventually the tension in the Scherz home relaxed to the point where the hostages moved around the house quite freely. Dr. Scherz explained, "I would say, 'Listen, I am going to my office' and he said, 'Doc, you go where you want. You know I don't worry where you are going.'"34

The doctor also explained that he felt the gunman was very concerned for the captives' safety. In the event the police stormed the house, "He told us to go into the two bedrooms. To cover ourselves with mattresses. He didn't want to hurt us." 35

Dr. Scherz's release on Wednesday was pivotal to the eventual resolution of the hostage-taking. The doctor promised to speak directly to the surgeon who operated on Dorothy Archer and to arrange for continuous communication between Archer and his lawyer. This provided the initial steps toward the final terms of surrender.

The *Winnipeg Free Press* then went on to remind its readers, "The hostages had not heard, however, that the gunman was wanted for questioning in connection with the death of a Calgary businessman. If they had, they would have talked to the gunman quite differently, Mrs. Scherz said."36

In his final dramatic statement to the press before gratefully heading home from the town hall, David Penny explained, "All the time we were in there I thought if I can walk out of here I'll just kiss the ground. But when we walked out I felt so dead inside."37

On Monday morning Herbert Archer appeared briefly before Judge F.W. Coward in Brandon's provincial judges' court. He was arraigned, jointly with his wife, on the murder of RCMP Constable Dennis Onofrey. Their lawyers entered pleas of not guilty on their behalves. Additional charges including kidnapping were postponed temporarily. Dorothy remained under guard in the Brandon General Hospital.

Archer waited in Headingly Correctional Institute with a surveillance camera trained on his maximum security cell until his trial began in Brandon on Wednesday, November 15, 1978. Dorothy was held at the Portage Correctional Institute for Women.

Lawyer Jay Prober acted on Dorothy Archer's behalf. Hersh Wolch continued to represent Herbert Archer. Jack Montgomery served as Crown counsel. They chose a nine-man, three-woman jury after rejecting more than one hundred and sixty potential jurors. 38

With Mr. Justice John M. Hunt of the Manitoba Court of Queen's Bench presiding in Brandon, the court case began with eye witness reports of the gun battle at the Countryside Inn, which had left two RCMP officers seriously injured and one dead. The testimonies added little that wasn't already known about the fatal altercation.

RCMP Constable Garry Harrison, who had accompanied Archer on his drive from Oak Lake to Brandon, read aloud his notes from the trip. Archer had explained to the Mountie: "The police came to the door, yelled and kicked open the door. I grabbed the gun. The police had their guns out. The cop on the right pulled back the hammer [on his gun] and I fired. I didn't see where it hit him." [39]

Harrison also told the court that "Archer also said he was sorry one of the officers had to die ... [and] absolved Dorothy Archer from any part of the incident and that any gun he had given her was unloaded." [40]

Considering the seriousness of the charges, authorities spent an inordinate amount of time determining the legal status of Dorothy and Herbert Archer's union. Crown counsel Montgomery asked that Dorothy be charged under the name Dorothy Malette as well as Dorothy Archer. The couple maintained they were married in Reno, Nevada, in 1975; however, Eldon Malette of Newcastle, Ontario, testified that he had married Dorothy on May 1, 1965, one week after her fifteenth birthday. To his knowledge they remained married.

Her lawyer, Jay Prober, objected to Crown counsel Montgomery's constant reference to his client as "Malette." In a masterpiece of redundancy, Montgomery informed the judge, "It is discourteous, rude, ungentlemanly, not professional and not fair to refer to her as Malette." He also asserted that "his client is a human being and is entitled to be called by what she says is her name." [41]

"Mr. Justice Hunt ruled that Prober's client was charged as Dorothy Archer, otherwise known as Dorothy Malette, and he wasn't going to restrict Montgomery's use of the name. However, the Crown attorney refrained from calling her Malette for the rest of the day ..." [42] Corporal Ken Bullock testified that, while being examined after the hostage-taking, Archer gave his occupation as "killer." He also spoke of finding Archer's fingerprints on items inside Unit 20 at the Countryside Inn.

The trial dragged on, with the presentation of technical details and photographs of the Scherz house, and the testaments of residents of the communities surrounding the crime. David Penny's wife, Irene, testified that the Archers threatened them with the fact they'd already killed a police officer and therefore had nothing to left to lose by killing again.

Despite this, Irene and David Penny's older daughter maintained, "Herbert Archer was gentle and apologized for everything."[43]

Those closest to Herbert Archer during the siege were the hostages themselves, and to a lesser degree, the police who were in almost constant telephone contact. Oddly, the testimony these people gave regarding the man's personality often appeared contradictory.

Dr. Scherz, who had some knowledge of psychology and psychiatry from his medical training, testified: "Archer appeared to be rational during the hostage-taking incident." [44]

The Scherzes also assured the court that Archer seemed a kind and considerate man who did not want to harm anyone.

RCMP Staff Sergeant Gerald Ferguson, however, disagreed. Ferguson stated that during his telephone conversations with Archer the previous January, the accused often seemed out of touch with reality.

Ferguson and his fellow officers also had difficulty accepting the scenario of Herbert Archer as a well-intentioned but unfortunate man. They saw a man who had shot three of their colleagues, killing one, and who had strangled Maurice Crystal.

Of the two polarities, the police likely held the more accurate assessment of the Archers. The powerful phenomenon of the Stockholm Syndrome no doubt played an important role in the hostages' calculations. Understandably they held a vested interest in the belief of their captor's innate goodness as a human being.

After assuring the jury that she had felt confident that Archer was both rational and kind, Stephanie Scherz described the trance-like states he experienced.

"His eyes rolled in his head and he was perspiring," she said.[45]

In this altered mental state Archer attempted to contact his wife, at the Brandon General Hospital, by mental telepathy. When he was unable to reach her, Archer determined that the doctors must have "doped" her.[46]

In recounting a more bizarre event, Stephanie Scherz explained to the jury that Archer once ranted, "I'm hot. I'm hot. My other self is coming through. Nobody can do anything but Dorothy. I'm not responsible for what I do. I speak Spanish when my other self comes out. You'll have to sing me a lullaby."[47]

When the episode had ended, Archer explained that he once suffered a "breakdown" and "spent seven months in a mental institution." Archer credited Dorothy with being responsible for his current mental soundness. She "nursed him like a baby back to full health."[48]

While an explanation will likely never be possible, Stephanie Scherz, perhaps unwittingly, summarized all of this contradictory information from the witness stand, when she explained, "The man in the house was not the same man the police knew."[49]

On Wednesday, December 6, after seventeen days of testimony by sixty-three witnesses, the lawyers in the case of *R vs Herbert and Dorothy Archer* prepared to deliver their summations.

Crown counsel Jack Montgomery delivered his to the jury "[i]n a style best described as a preacher and a politician." The "fiery faced" [50] Montgomery insisted that Dorothy Archer was every bit as guilty as her husband in the murder of Constable Dennis Onofrey.

"The two ... formed a common intention to avoid arrest in connection with criminal charges in British Columbia." Further, Montgomery reminded the jury that after knocking on the door of Room 20 at the Countryside Inn the RCMP officers identified themselves as police. The Archers knew they weren't being attacked by criminals.[51]

Brian Cole, reporter for the *Winnipeg Free Press*, explained the lawyer's premise this way: "Mrs. Archer knew, or ought to have known, that the shooting of a police officer could be the consequence of the decision to resist arrest." [52]

In conclusion Jack Montgomery, anticipating his colleague's tactics, recommended that the jury "be cautious about any self-defence theory presented by Hersh Wolch."[53]

Dorothy Archer's lawyer, Jay Prober, took great pains both verbally and physically to separate his client from her husband. While giving his summation, he frequently stood between the jury and Herbert Archer. By blocking their view of the man who killed the Mountie and leaving only Dorothy Archer to look at, he hoped to increase sympathy for the woman. He maintained Dorothy's innocence and reminded the jury that the woman "was behind a screen in the motel [bath]room at the time of the shooting and never fired a shot."[54]

Prober demonstrated a keen memory and a flare for the dramatic by addressing several of the jurors personally, by name. "Mr. Goodman, you said you wanted to hear the other side of the story. As did you Wilbur Fingus and as did you Dennis Magwood," said in reference to comments the men made many weeks before, during the jury selection process.

"You have [now] heard the other side. You should acquit the accused," he asserted with finality. [55]

Hersh Wolch, Herbert Archer's lawyer, proposed that the RCMP, not his client, was to blame in the constable's death. He maintained the police "mishandled the stolen vehicle investigation which led to the shootings ... [and that] the entire matter was handled with no planning or direction." [56]

Wolch suggested that while his client might be guilty of using excessive force in self-defence, that only constitutes a charge of manslaughter, not first-degree murder for which he was currently being tried. He concluded by adopting Stephanie Scherz's philosophy that Herbert Archer "was a good man caught in unforeseeable circumstances."[57]

Mr. Justice Hunt's summation relied heavily on the definition of "common intent" as "a plan by two or more parties for an unlawful purpose, in this case to avoid arrest. If murder was a probable consequence of the common plan to resist arrest, both parties were guilty," he advised the jury.[58]

At one o'clock the jury retired to review the summations and all the evidence presented to them since the case had begun on November 15, 1978. In keeping with courtroom custom, all three lawyers addressed Mr. Justice John M. Hunt regarding his summation. Both defence lawyers soundly criticized the Court of Queen's Bench judge. Wolch suggested the judge came "close to directing the jury to finding a guilty verdict" by "highlighting features the Crown had forgotten." This premise included a reminder "that the Archers didn't have to open their motel room door if they thought the people knocking were thugs. He said one could question as to why Archer opened the door at all. He could have phoned the manager and said there are thugs outside."[59]

Dorothy Archer's lawyer, Jay Prober, objected to the judge's comparison of the Archers to Bonnie and Clyde. This, he suggested "was injudicious, most unfair and tainted, particularly from Mrs. Archer's point of view. It conjured up an image of a couple on a rampage — of shooting and robbing."[60]

Crown counsel Jack Montgomery, however, had nothing but praise for the judge's words and called his charge "exemplary."[61]

On Saturday, December 9, 1978, at 11:50 a.m., after seven and a half hours' deliberation, the jury foreman, Donald Hicks, advised the court of their unanimous decision. They found Herbert and Dorothy Archer guilty of first-degree murder.

Herbert Archer responded by telling the court, "I'd like to inform everybody in the court right now that I am not guilty of first-degree murder. True, I took a life and I'm sorry about that. But if I have to spend the rest of my life in prison for saving the life of my wife, I will gladly do it."[62]

Dorothy Archer, not quite as eloquent or magnanimous as her husband merely sobbed, "It's not fair. I didn't do anything."[63]

Hersh Wolch announced that he would start appeal proceedings immediately. He cited "at least ten strong grounds and ten less significant grounds for appeal."[64]

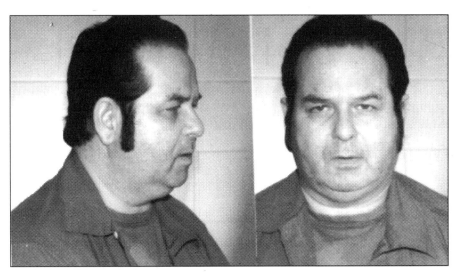

Herbert Bruce Archer

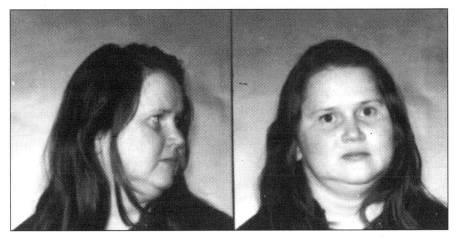

Dorothy Malette (alias Dorothy Archer)

Emotions ran high. The *Winnipeg Free Press* reported, "Several RCMP officers shook hands and patted each other on the back as though they had just won a football game." They went on to note, "Several jurors broke down and cried." Even Jay Prober, Dorothy Archer's lawyer, was "visibly shaken."[65]

Mr. Justice John Hunt issued the only sentence available under the circumstances. He sentenced both Herbert and Dorothy Archer to "mandatory life imprisonment with no parole for twenty-five years."[66]

Hunt set January 15, 1979, as the date on which the Archers would face the lesser charges of kidnapping and unlawful confinement. Ten days before that, however, Herbert Archer made the front page of the *Winnipeg Free Press* again.

Disagreements between Archer and the guards at Headingly Correctional Institute escalated. Archer's threats to "get someone" [67] eventually became physical, and medical attention was needed to treat a three-inch cut in his head. After having the gash sutured, Archer was transferred, under heavy guard to Stony Mountain Penitentiary to await his second court hearing.

Meanwhile, Dorothy Archer waited, somewhat more quietly, in the women's prison.

In the end, the judge ruled that Herbert Archer would serve twelve years and Dorothy Archer ten years concurrently with their life sentences.[68]

Despite Hersh Wolch's confidence about easily obtaining an appeal, he never succeeded in arranging one.

Herbert Archer, perhaps sensing that this might be his last opportunity to speak publicly about his guilt or innocence made a long statement to the press: "Why did it happen? I still can't answer. It happened so suddenly. This whole episode started with fright. I was scared to death. I knew I was being chased by a multitude of police who were out to kill me and my wife. All I could hear [in his mind] was them yelling 'shoot him, kill him.' I was just trying to survive. I was trying to save me and my wife."

The apparently humbled Archer concluded with a plea for sympathy by pleading a poor image: "I've been made to look like a real criminal, which I've never been."[69]

The Archers never did stand trial for Maurice Crystal's murder. The Calgary police had travelled to Manitoba and charged the couple; however, the charges were stayed.

Today, the couple continue to serve their sentences in separate jails. They are scheduled for release in the year 2003.

NO FOOL LIKE AN OLD FOOL

L ife in the Canadian Maritimes during the early days of this century was usually peaceful; wildlife roamed plentifully, and lakes and bubbling streams sparkled. Even daily newspapers were different then.

The following short article appeared in the *Halifax Herald* in a prominent front-page spot, apparently unconnected to any news story, on Wednesday, August 30, 1922. The words merely ran as information worthy of print.

KEMPTVILLE

The village of Kemptville, which has a population of 500 souls, is situated in a famous hunting and fishing region in Yarmouth County, twenty-eight miles from the town of Yarmouth. The nearest railway station is at Brazil Lake, twelve miles away on the Dominion Atlantic line. The nearest telegraph and express offices are situated at Brazil Lake. A daily mail coach runs from the station to the village.

Kemptville village contains two stores, an hotel, two sawmills, a telephone office and a Baptist church. The surrounding country is studded with lakes and lined with small streams. These, with the headwaters of the Tusket River, provide some of the best trout and salmon fishing in the province. The region is also a favorite feeding ground of moose, fox and lynx. [1]

Across the masthead, the *Halifax Herald* proclaimed its motto and philosophy: "Truth — Justice" and "Open to Reason." The publisher tucked the paper's ambitious mandate, "First in Everything," on the second page. The *Halifax Herald* served its 1920s readers with a distinct and dramatic flair.

Those readers included the citizens of Kemptville, two hundred kilometers, as the crow flies, from Halifax. The descriptive paragraphs carried by the newspaper only hinted at the natural beauty of the community: the "best trout and salmon fishing in the province" and "favourite feeding ground of moose, fox and lynx" combined to give the area a lucrative tourist industry, thanks to wealthy American sport hunters.

Kemptville was so serene a town (unless you were a hunter's target) that the setting of a Norman Rockwell painting looks threatening by comparison. Each of the 500 citizens knew each other, and many married their fellow townsfolk, creating even stronger ties. What affected one household usually touched the lives of most of the others.

In the late 1800s, Omar Roberts, owner of Riverside House, a prosperous hunting and fishing lodge, married the fair, young Randall, girl, sister of Robert and William Randall. The union pleased both families, and the marriage lasted until her death in September 1921. All who knew her mourned the woman's passing but once the shock subsided, both families realized some arrangement would have to be made to have the domestic duties at Riverside House carried out. Only one of the Roberts's children, a daughter, remained at home. She, "although not half-wited [sic] appeared somewhat defective mentally."[2] This condition ruled out Roberts's daughter taking over the functions previously performed by her mother.

Mr. and Mrs. Clarence Gray immediately offered the services of their teenage daughter, Flora. Despite being bright, physically attractive, and well trained in domestic matters, Flora had remained unmarried. Most in the town agreed she'd do a fine job as the housekeeper for the widower Roberts. The Grays and Omar Roberts struck a deal, and Flora left her parents' home to take up residence in the north wing of Riverside House.

A comfortable routine soon established itself and, before long, life in Kemptville returned to normal. There was never any gossip about the arrangement, despite Flora being of marriageable age and Roberts once again being single. They did live in different parts of the house, and Omar Roberts, at sixty-eight, was not a young man.

Roberts passed the first winter without his wife quietly. By the arrival of spring he had come to grips with his loss and had begun to notice more of the world around him. He returned to his duties as host and hunting guide, and he also began to notice Flora Gray. Omar Roberts admired the young girl's efficiency around Riverside House, her cheery disposition and her pleasing appearance. Not long after noticing these endearing qualities, the old man's fancy turned to love.

"Come with me for a canoe ride on the river, Flora," he suggested one afternoon in mid August. "I need to find out how far downstream the moose are and I'd like your help with noting landmarks."

With so many varied duties, this request didn't strike Flora as being suspect. She packed a picnic lunch for two in the wicker hamper and joined her employer at the dock where he kept his canoe.

But they'd been out on the water only a few minutes when Omar began to speak: "Flora, you've been a wonderful help to me. I want you to know I appreciate that very much."

The young woman stared uncomprehendingly for a moment. Not only had she never heard Roberts speak this way, but she'd been temporarily lost in a daydream, for she too had been caught by a late-summer case of spring fever. The object of Flora Gray's affections, however, was not Omar Roberts. Gray viewed Omar as nothing more than her elderly employer; it was young Ransom Randall who'd captured Flora's attention.

The strapping sixteen-year-old lived with his parents, Mr. and Mrs. William Randall: Omar's wife had been the young man's aunt, his father's sister. The Randalls' property abutted Roberts's, and the couple frequently invited the old man to their home after his wife's death. Roberts often brought young Flora along on these visits, unwittingly giving romance an opportunity to blossom. And so, on the sunny afternoon of their canoe trip together, Omar and Flora operated with very different agendas. Neither had any idea the other had fallen for someone younger than themselves.

Into this cauldron of intense emotions, Omar Roberts threw a marriage proposal. It took a measurable few seconds for the words to register with Flora, and so he repeated his entreaty: "Please, Flora, will you be my wife?"

Although he was well aware that Flora was nearly fifty years his junior, he also knew that both socially and materially he could offer a great deal to the young woman. Few men were as highly regarded in the community. By marrying Omar, Flora would share that elevated social standing.

Flora Gray, however, apparently didn't aspire to such worldly heights. Her ambitions lay no further than the virile Ransom Randall.

"Mr. Roberts," Flora replied in shock. "How can you say that? How can you suggest such a thing? You're rude. I demand that you take me back to shore."

Omar Roberts tried hard to convince Flora that he hadn't suggested anything that might tarnish her reputation. But the more Omar cajoled her the more Flora edged toward hysteria.

"All right, all right," he conceded at last. "I'll take you back to the dock on one condition. You must never tell anyone about this conversation. It will be our secret. Can you at least agree to that, Flora?"

The relieved girl nodded, and a badly disappointed Omar Roberts turned the canoe toward shore.

As good as her word, Flora Gray told no one of her employer's proposal. Her silence wasn't as much motivated by loyalty as practicalities. Who would she have told? Perhaps her mother, if the woman had still been alive, but certainly not her father or step-mother. They would be sure she'd been behaving in evil ways in order to give a highly respected man like Omar Roberts such ideas. She pushed the memory of the canoe trip to the far recesses of her mind.

One beautiful day led to another that August of 1922. The world enjoyed renewed economic prosperity after the horrors of the First World War; Riverside House received a steady stream of guests; and the marriage proposal was not mentioned by the only two who knew about it. Time passed pleasantly, with routine work during the day and socializing after supper. And so it was that on the evening of August 28, Omar Roberts and Flora Gray walked to the Randalls' home for an early evening visit.

Omar went into the house while Flora stayed out on the verandah with some young people who'd gathered there. The sounds of the youngsters' laughter drifted through the Randalls' open doors and windows.

By ten o'clock Roberts decided to say good night to the Randalls. He went outside, expecting to walk home with Flora, but much to his surprise and displeasure she wasn't there.

"Ransom walked her home," one of the remaining youths offered.

"I see," Omar nodded.

William Randall and his wife prepared for bed. Glancing out the livingroom window before closing the drapes, William noted the lights in his brother's home, just a few yards away, still shone. Robert and Jessie, his wife, must still be awake, he reflected, staring out onto the otherwise darkened horizon. Then, much to his surprise an automobile came into view — Omar's automobile to be exact. Omar steered the car across the Randalls' lawn, waving his hand out the window.

"Hurry! Hurry!" Roberts exhorted as he brought his car to a stop at the bottom step of the Randalls' verandah. "It may be too late. Flora may already be gone."

"My good god man," William Randall implored as he raced outside. "What do you mean Flora's gone. Where?"

Robert Randall heard the commotion across the lawn and hurried to his brother's side. Their wives followed only seconds later.

"There's been a terrible fire in the house," Roberts explained while urging the four into his car. "Poor dear Flora must have started it accidentally. I tried to get to her but the heat from the flames kept me back. I fear she's gone. Dead."

Finally comprehending the emergency at hand, William Randall joined Omar Roberts in his automobile.

"Robert, round up some others and meet us at Omar's," he ordered before turning to his wife. "You and Jessie send someone to town in a car to phone for help."

The former proved unnecessary. The flames, the smoke and the unaccustomed commotion had brought neighbours from miles around. They quickly

organized a bucket brigade from the river to Riverside House and soon
brought the blaze under control. Young Ransom Randall led the party of rescuers up the stairs of the badly damaged north wing.

At first glance he was sure his beloved Flora lay dead before his eyes. The
sight of the young woman's crumpled body and the acrid smell of burned
flesh held Ransom and the others rooted in the doorway. Surely he'd arrived
too late. Ransom took off his shirt to cover as much of her exposed body as he
could. He could at least save her dignity and modesty.

As Ransom covered her face Flora moved slightly and made a small, ani-
mal-like sound.

"My god, she's alive!" he exclaimed. "Help me move her. We've got to get
her out of here. The fire could start up again any minute."

William Randall moved forward to help his son. Fighting revulsion at the
sight and smell of the dying girl, he knelt to help carry Flora to safety. Oddly,
she seemed to be trying to talk, to tell him something.

Once outside, they laid her carefully on the seat of Robert Randall's car.

"Take her to my house," William ordered. "Help's on its way."

As the car pulled away, those left behind heard an ominous crackling from
the upper storey of Riverside House. The fire they thought was extinguished
had re-ignited with a vengeance. Before they could re-organize the line of men
from the river to the fire, the timbers gave way and the burning house collapsed in on itself. Omar Roberts watched in silence as his once proud and
happy home and lodge became a pile of ashes.

The neighbour conscripted to drive to a telephone elected to make only
one phone call. Oddly, rather than calling James McMellon,[3] Kemptville's
only police officer, he called the town's postmaster, a man named Gates.

Within minutes of the call, Gates forwarded the following message to
Crown prosecutor McKay: "Send officer immediately to investigate and take
action."[4] Evidently McKay felt that this was a matter the town cop should at
least be involved in, because within the hour, he and policeman James
McMellon joined the growing cluster of men at the smoldering remains of
Riverside House.

"Is anyone in there?" McMellon shouted over the din of the crowd.

"Not now," came the reply from the centre of a knot of onlookers.

"Omar's housekeeper was in there. She must have started the fire. We got
her out but I doubt she's still alive. Pretty badly burned up, so she was,"
William Roberts explained, breaking away from the group to address the
policeman. "They took her to my house and called Dr. Farish, though I doubt
there'd be much he could do."

"I'm going over there to check on the girl," McMellon informed Gates.
He recognized the uncomfortable feeling which grew deep in the pit of his

stomach. Through his years of experience as a police officer, he'd learned to trust his intuitions. McMellon abruptly turned his back on the crowd and the ruins of Riverside House.

Robert Randall's wife greeted him on the verandah.

"Oh, James, it's dreadful, just awful, the poor lass, she's burned so bad it pains me to look at her," Jessie sobbed as she ushered the police officer into her brother-in-law's house. "Dr. Farish is with her. I don't know if he'll let you see her. We've called for her parents. The doctor may want the girl to save her energy for her good-byes to them before she joins her sainted mother in the hereafter."

"The law will come before family in this case, I'm afraid, Mrs. Randall, but I do appreciate your concern. Now show me where you have the girl."

Although fully three feet from the door to the parlor, James McMellon knew where Flora Gray lay. The stench of burned flesh sent waves of nausea through his body. As he paused at the doorway and fought for control, a hand shoved him aside and a couple brushed passed him into the parlor.

Unused to being treated with such a lack of respect, McMellon understood seconds later when he recognized Flora's father kneeling beside the blackened body.

The officer moved quietly up beside Flora's distraught step-mother, who had stationed herself behind her kneeling husband, Clarence.

For a long while the youngster lay immobile and silent, but perhaps sensing her father's presence, she struggled to consciousness.

"Mr. Roberts," she murmured barely audibly.

"Mr. Roberts?" her father probed. "You want to see Omar Roberts?"

A thin high-pitched sound came from the fatally injured, young woman's throat and she made a painful attempt to turn her head. Omar Roberts's name appeared to fill Flora with revulsion. Still turned away, and now gasping for air, the young woman tried again to relay the information she knew she had only minutes left to share.

"No," the dying girl gasped. She took several raspy breaths before finding the strength to continue, "... gasoline on the floor ... tried to fight him, Papa."

Clarence Gray gasped and looked toward his wife for support. She spoke to the girl.

"Flora, that can't be so. Why would a man like Omar Roberts do such a thing? You must be mistaken," the older woman chastised.

Although her voice was nearly inaudible by now, anger tinged the dying young woman's reply.

"... would not marry him."

The disclosure robbed Flora Gray of her final breath. Her charred body succumbed to the ravages of the burns. With a final rush of foul-smelling breath, Flora closed her eyes and claimed her final reward.

The odd cluster of people in Robert Randall's parlor fell still and silent for a moment. As Farish, the town doctor, moved to cover the body, the others began backing away from the chaise on which the corpse lay.

"I'm going to get Omar Roberts," James McMellon announced to no one in particular as he left the Randalls' house.

Dr. Farish finished covering the body, relieved that the young woman was freed from her suffering. He knew she had no chance of recovering from such extensive damage. Her feet had been burned to the bone. The man cringed when he thought how much the child had suffered. There would have to be an autopsy. He asked one of the neighbours who had gathered on the verandah to drive into town and bring Dr. S.W. Williamson back to assist him with the postmortem examination and to notify Dr. A.R. Melanson that his services would also be needed. In addition to being the coroner for the Kemptville area of Nova Scotia, Melanson was also the area's Provincial Member of Parliament.

Melanson arrived at the scene of the murder before daybreak and immediately began preparing to conduct a coroner's inquest. This man did not like to waste time. According to the Wednesday, August 30th, issue of the *Halifax Herald*, he "immediately upon his arrival made arrangements to summon a jury." Obviously Melanson completed his arrangements with remarkable efficiency because the newspaper goes on to report, "The inquest commenced at about eleven-thirty this forenoon and continued all day and well into this evening." [5]

Officer McMellon stayed for the proceedings and requested that Omar Roberts wait with him.

Postmaster Gates served as the jury foreman. The balance of the group consisted of assorted Kemptville men: Leslie Prosser, Harvey Prosser, Charles Crowell, Lawrence Munro, Stanley Raynard, Gilbert Walton, Albert Ring, Lloyd Ring, Bradford Ring, C.R. Reeves and Avard Gates.

After a viewing of the remains by all present, the duly appointed men of the jury heard a stream of witnesses repeat their version of the events which had led up to and followed Flora Gray's death.

Dr. Williamson gave his expert opinion that burns of that extent couldn't have been caused merely by burning cloth or wood, but must have been accelerated by a substance such as gasoline. Some neighbours reported trying to extinguish the fire; others spoke of listening in horror as Flora Gray accused her employer, the inestimable Omar Roberts, of killing her. Still others retold how they impotently watched the hideously burned teenager's body give up its struggle.

When the inquest adjourned, Undertaker Sweeney took the body to prepare it for burial. By nine o'clock Wednesday evening, less than two days after the death, the jury issued the following statement:

> We, the jury chosen to enquire into the death of Flora Gray, after having the witnesses sworn on oath and whose evidence is herewith attached, say that the said Flora Gray came to her death on August 29th, 1922, at ... Robert Randall's, North Kemptville, Yarmouth County, Nova Scotia, by shock caused by severe burning, received at Omar Roberts' house on the night of August 28th, 1922. The said burns were caused by gasoline or some other inflammable substance spread on the floor of her room, and ignited, and as she and Omar Roberts were the only ones in the house at that time, as evidence points to him as having perpetrated the crime, we come to the conclusion that Omar Roberts was the cause of her death. [6]

Officer James McMellon drove the accused to a Yarmouth cell. He would be arraigned before Magistrate Charles Pelton later in the day.

Well aware of his privileged standing in the community and knowing that the findings of a coroner's inquest were not sufficient to condemn him, Omar Roberts plotted possible strategies for his trial.

"Did she regain consciousness?" Roberts probed during the drive.

"Yes," replied Constable McMellon, "and she told the whole story." [7]

"So you know?"

"Yes," the constable echoed.

The years since 1922 have altered journalistic styles a great deal. By present-day standards, the *Halifax Herald's* coverage seems tastelessly melodramatic. Even the paper's initial headline regarding the crime sounds strange in light of modern prose. The banner read: "SHOCKING TRAGEDY NEAR YARMOUTH"[8] — leaving the reader to wonder what tragedy would not be shocking.

In slightly smaller print, readers are advised: "Flora Gray, Dying from Burns, Charges Man with Encompassing Her Death." The article goes on to report:

> A beautiful innocent girl's life snuffed out, homes in sorrow and anguish, an erstwhile honored and respected man lodged in gaol and resting under the shadow of a frightful crime,

Halifax Herald, Wednesday, August 30, 1922 (Shocking Tragedy Near Yarmouth). (Courtesy of the Halifax *Chronicle-Herald*.)

sums up the awful tragedy which took place under the cover of night at beautiful North Kemptville, the fairest of the many beautiful hamlets in this county of Yarmouth. Horror unspeakable fills the hearts and minds of the people of this county today while over the fair group of villages known as Kemptville East and North Kemptville hangs a pall of sorrow blacker than night. 9

The following day, Thursday, August 31, 1922, the case shared headline space with international news, although the local story rated a larger and more prominent placement. In varying sizes of print above the story of the fire victim's funeral, the following was noted for the readers:

Pathetic Scenes At Funeral Of Flora Gray. Funeral Of Flora Gray Took Place Yesterday: Scenes of Deepest Grief At Graveside. Remains of Unfortunate Girl Cruelly Brought to Her Death Were Interred at Kemptville — Grief Stricken Family Pathetic Figures, Omar Roberts, Charged With Murder, Presented Broken Appearance at Preliminary

Hearing — Unrepresented By Counsel — Tributes to
Heroism Of Kemptville Men. [10]

While the style of reporting has changed dramatically over the years,
many of the issues reported on have not. The following information ran
between the report the movements of French troops along the border of
France and Germany of Flora's funeral and:

Provincial Governments Criticized By Premier. Tendency To
Shelve Responsibility On Federal Government Sharply
Denounced. Prime Minister Charges Opposition Leader
With Harboring Ill-Will and Bitterness. [11]

Omar Roberts thought little about any events other than his own predica-
ment. His feet had been severely burned in the fatal fire. The excruciating
pain meant he thought of little other than his own suffering, although he
clearly realized he'd been accused of murder.

"The silly wench didn't have an iota of common sense. If she had she'd
have pounced at the chance to marry me," the incarcerated Roberts decided.
"If people knew they'd understand, I'm sure. Imagine, turning down my marriage proposal just to endure the childish pantings of that Ransom Randall."

Roberts still found it inconceivable to think that Flora had turned down
his proposal merely because she did not want to marry him. His egocentric
mind apparently rationalized that it could only have been Flora's attraction to
another that would prohibit her from accepting his generous offer.

Over and over again Roberts reviewed the events leading up to the fire,
including those humiliating nervous giggles from the teenagers gathered that
evening on William Randall's verandah.

"Ransom walked her home," one of them had shouted in reply to his
query about where his housekeeper was. Now, at last, he knew the object of
her affections. Barely able to control himself he had hurried toward Riverside
House, his ire building with each step.

"If they're there together I'll kill them both," he determined, shaking with
rage at the thought of the two defiling his property. Riverside House stood for
all Omar's hard work and accomplishments. He couldn't bear to think of it as
the setting for Flora's passion, especially after she had abruptly rejected his plea
mere weeks before.

As he approached the house, Omar could hardly believe his eyes: the
chairs on the porch stood empty.

"The filthy hussy has taken that boy into my home," he deduced, incor-
rectly.

"Flora! Flora!" he screamed as he entered the house. "You can't hide from me. I know you two are in there together. I'll get both of you."

As she had undressed in preparation for bed upstairs, her employer's threats had finally broke through Flora's reverie. She had recognized Omar's voice but couldn't understand why he was shouting. Her mind was still on Ransom. He'd held her hand for the first time this evening and squeezed it meaningfully before taking his leave just moments before. A contented smile remained on the pretty young woman's slightly flushed face. Omar Roberts was far from her mind and so, for a few seconds, his rantings made no sense to her. Those few seconds Flora Gray spent urging her mind away from its daydream proved to be fatal. By fleeing Riverside House the moment she heard Roberts's voice, she might have saved her life — and his too; however, fear and confusion combined to immobilize her.

Roberts's obscene threats filled the air. The door to her bedroom burst open. For a moment Flora thought she even smelled his anger. Too late she realized the odour came from the bucket of gasoline he carried. When she tried to run past the old man, a sudden stab of pain in her eyes stopped her. As her hand flew to her eyes, a wave of gasoline cascaded down the side of her face. Flora watched the blurred image of her employer retreating from her room to the landing outside her bedroom door. A trail of petrol followed him: it linked their two lives permanently, but not in the way Omar Roberts had envisioned that afternoon on the lake.

He knocked the coal oil lamp off its stand just outside her bedroom and dumped the last few ounces of gas on the floor at the top of the staircase, spilling some on his own feet. Seconds later the flame from the lamp touched the puddles of gasoline, and Roberts stood transfixed — even while fire seered his own flesh.

Flora screamed as she fell to her bed, writhing, engulfed in flames. He knew she would die. He intended her to. But he didn't intend for her to live as long as she did — long enough to implicate him in her murder.

Townsfolk in and around Kemptville spoke of little else. Everyone knew Roberts. Most respected him. The man's age and previous standing in the community contradicted the senseless and barbaric crime. Most also knew young Flora Gray and, perhaps in keeping with accepted social customs, no one could think of a bad word to say about the young woman. Presumably all were reassured when they read "that Flora Gray died with her honor untarnished." [12]

That important issue dealt with, all that remained was Omar Roberts's trial on the charge of murder.

Dozens of curious citizens milled around the Yarmouth courthouse early Wednesday morning, September 6, 1922. Magistrate Charles Pelton barred all but "press representatives and those directly concerned with the proceedings."[13] This meant replacing the freelance writer who had been covering the case for the *Herald*, with a "Staff Correspondent." Perhaps the freelancer then applied his journalistic talents to the following intriguing headlines in the Wednesday, September 6, 1922, edition, in which "Special to the Herald" (a journalistic term to indicate work done by someone other than regular staff) started a story about "John Merritt, Sidney Mines, Still Missing: Theory Obtains He Might Have Been Seized By a Monster Fish at Lloyd's Cove." [14]

The less flamboyant but regular staff writer explained the switch in reporters by adding, "Even witnesses will be admitted to the court room one by one as they are called." [15]

Omar Roberts sat alone at a table near the front of the room. His conversation with Constable McMellon in the latter's car had been accepted as an admission of guilt. The anguish showed on the old man's features, and many witnesses gasped in shock as they took their place on the stand and glanced at Roberts's once proud features.

The staff correspondent for the *Halifax Herald* reminded the paper's readers that the, "prompt action of Mr. MacKay, [Crown prosecutor] immediately following the tragedy in taking matters in hand, having the accused lodged in jail here, of clearing everything away to a verdict from the coroner's jury on the same day on which the crime was reported to him, is action that has possibly established a record in this province." [16]

The writer goes on to remind readers that in addition to the scene of the crime being a considerable distance (thirty miles) from Yarmouth, the "work was done in the pouring rain." [17] Obviously not a man to let adversity slow him down, Crown prosecutor McKay predicted the trial would take only a day.

Despite the apparently cut-and-dried nature of the case, the *Herald* reporter reminded those who may have forgotten that the due course of the legal proceedings would still be followed.

"There seems to be a prevailing opinion that, with an admission of guilt in the hands of the authorities, further evidence will not be necessary. This, of course, is an erroneous impression. Statements of this nature are accepted as evidence along with the other evidence detailing the particulars of the tragedy, before and after the fact."[18]

The witnesses from the coroner's inquest stood by, ready to repeat their testimony, and, in addition, Flora's father, Clarence Gray, and her uncle Judson Gray were expected to be called to testify. Yarmouth lawyer, R.W.E. Landry, K.C., represented the interests of the deceased girl's family.

No one wished for a quick trial more than the accused. Omar Roberts expressed his unrequited love for the late Flora Gray and "pity"[19] for her grieving father. Displaying severely degenerated mental health, Roberts also explained that he held Flora blameless despite her rejection of him being the aggravating cause of his current situation.

He demonstrated this skewed mental state with an almost panicked concern at the possibility that both his badly burned feet might need to be amputated — a strange worry for a man whose guilty plea would inevitably lead to his execution.

Hobbling on bandaged feet, the decrepit-looking old man made his way to the witness stand, following those who'd now given their testimony twice — first at the coroner's inquest and now, here. Roberts explained that his lethal actions occurred "after this fit of passion took me." [20]

> I think I went and got a bucket and some gasoline out of a barrel. I went to the end of the house and saw the light still burning in Flora's room. I think I went in the back door and upstairs. I think I set the bucket on the outside of the door that led into her room. I think she asked me if I was crazy: I think my reply was, I think I am. I think she walked around the bed which was close to the door, and I went out and got the gasoline, and ... threw it on her and on the bed ... I knocked the lamp off to set it afire. The lamp was lighted while I was in the room and then I dodged out of the room. I cannot think whether I lighted a match or not. I saw a flash in the room before I went out and I heard her scream. [21]

"Sir, whatever occurred to have caused you to feel such jealousy?" the Crown prosecutor asked the accused.

"It was the week before last that I was out on a canoe trip alone with Flora and then I asked her if she would have me. She replied that she thought I was too old. I thought a great deal of her and it was jealousy of the younger men that made me act and do what I did." Roberts replied.[22]

During further questioning, Omar Roberts defined the object of his jealousy more specifically as Ransom Randall, the fifteen-year-old son of his neighbour, Robert Randall.

Fittingly, Ransom Randall was the next witness to be called to the stand: "less than sixteen years, a clean-cut boy, straight as a lance, with fresh coloring, and the bearing of a man ten years his senior."[23]

With the introduction of this element, the *Herald's* writer found himself with a situation he relished. While the scribe's name may be lost to history, his literary enthusiasm is left for all to appreciate.

"As I watched the boy giving evidence, and heard him tell of Roberts' 'lack of sociability' on account of the lad's intimacy with Flora, only one thought could have flashed through my mind as it did — 'youth will be served.' Old Omar Roberts, much older than that boy's father, much older than the father of the girl on whom his aged affections were lavished — the spectacle of the broken old man, a pathetic heap like a heap of old clothes in the corner of the long dock, while Ransom Randall gave testimony to youthful affections and incongruous rivalry between him and a man old enough to be his grandfather ... this impossible rivalry out of which grew the jealousy and the passion that tore the breast of that human derelict who occupies a cell at the county jail tonight." [24]

Somewhat buried under the journalist's flowery prose, Ransom Randall's testimony endorsed the accused's motive and sealed the old man's fate. Before sundown, Omar Roberts learned that in a matter of weeks he would be hanged in the Yarmouth County Jail.

The end of the trial meant the drama that had held a corner of a Canadian province in virtual paralysis for nine days was over. Within hours, townsfolk and villagers returned to their regular activities and attended to matters which had been suspended during the tragedy and the ensuing excitement.

The murder affected every family in the Kemptville area, in varying degrees. Some families returned to lives badly scarred by the horror.

Clarence Gray grieved deeply for his only daughter. Ransom Randall pined for the girl he loved, and Roberts's daughter prepared herself for the death of her father.

For Omar Roberts, there could be no life to return to. The ruins of his beloved Riverside House reflected what was left. He could only prepare himself for his execution and to meet his maker.

The dawn of Friday, November 24, 1922, was grey and chilly. Sheriff Lewis led a worn but composed Omar Roberts from the cell where he'd spent his last hours with a clergyman in prayer and song. Roberts thanked the minister for his companionship and assured him "that if the execution would be the means of causing any nervous shock, he would not urge them to attend as he felt his strength sufficient and his faith in God of such great measure that he will go forward to his death without a fear." [25]

Despite Roberts's compassion, two clergymen, Rev. Dr. Edwin Crowell, a retired pastor of the Church of Kemptville, and M.S. Richardson, pastor of

Zion United Baptist Church in Yarmouth, stayed to witness the hanging. The date of the execution had been kept a secret and so, in addition to the ministers, only the prison physician, Sheriff Lewis, Jailer Sims, and "an unknown assistant" [26] watched as the trapdoor beneath Omar Roberts's feet swung fatally away.

SUMMER OF CARNAGE

George Bentley wondered how well he would adjust to retirement. He liked his job at the lumber mill near his home in Port Coquitlam, British Columbia, and took pride in the living he'd been able to provide for his family over the years. Once their kids grew up and established their own families George's wages didn't have to stretch nearly as far. He and his wife, Edith, enjoyed considerably more financial freedom than ever before.

Then a heart attack threatened George Bentley's ability to work. He worried. Would he and Edith be able to live comfortably on only his pension? The situation didn't concern the hardworking man for long. As soon as he recuperated, George realized that he and Edith were now completely at liberty to live the lives they'd always wanted to. He gave his notice at work, bought a new pickup truck and outfitted it with a camper. Their boat and motor fit nicely on the roof. They had, in a most portable fashion, all the comforts of home and complete freedom thrown in for good measure. What could be better?

Winters on Canada's southwest coast are balmy compared to the rest of the country; even so, the Bentleys relished the thought of exploring the southern States during the winter months. With a promise to keep in close touch, they locked up their home, asked several neighbours of long standing to keep an eye on things for them, and headed for the open road.

The only drawback Edith and George anticipated would be missing their family, especially their beloved grandchildren. They managed to keep up-to-date on the youngsters' activities by phoning either their son, Brian, and his family or their daughter, Jackie, and her family every week.

By spring of 1982, many of these phone calls revolved around plans to meet Jackie, her husband, Bob Johnson, and their two daughters, Janet and Karen, for a week's camping holiday. The Bentleys would head north to Canada and meet the younger couple and the children at Wells Gray Provincial Park in south central British Columbia. Neither the rugged terrain nor the isolation bothered any of the six. All were seasoned campers, well aware of how to enjoy the wilds safely.

Bob Johnson arranged for his holidays from work well in advance. His employers and fellow employees liked and admired Bob very much. After twenty-five years loyal service at Gorman Brothers Lumber Mill in Kelowna, he had earned his way to the position of chief sawyer — and he took pride in only ever missing a handful of days of work during all those years.

And so, at the beginning of August 1982, Bob Johnson, his wife and daughters all eagerly anticipated their annual family vacation. They packed their late-model Dodge Caravelle and made their way, through the mountains, first to visit friends in Red Deer, Alberta, and then a few days later, they reversed the scenic drive in order to rendezvous with Jackie's parents in the wilderness of Wells Gray Park.

The two little girls were especially excited. They could hardly wait to trade the restraints of city life for the freedom of camping. And, of course, they could hardly wait to see their grandparents George and Edith Bentley.

Well south and west of the park, amateur pilot Jaroslaw Ambrozuk, or Jerry as he preferred being called, was formulating a plan. The nineteen year old felt bored and confined by his life. Many young men would have counted themselves fortunate to have what Jerry did. The recent high-school graduate was an accomplished athlete, had lots of friends, a pretty girlfriend, and plans for a promising future. He first wanted to study geography at Simon Fraser University; eventually he wanted to be a pilot.

Jerry Ambrozuk's parents had a sincere interest in his welfare. But rather than giving the young man a sense of security, all these factors joined together to make him feel suffocated. He wanted to escape from his life in the Vancouver suburb of Burnaby. As yet, however, he just wasn't sure how or where he'd execute this escape.

Diane Babcock, Jerry's girlfriend of over a year's standing, didn't share his claustrophobia, but like most teenage girls she was eager for adventure. Her nursing studies at the British Columbia Institute of Technology were interesting but not nearly as exciting as the possibility of running away with Jerry.

In Hope, one hundred and fifty kilometres northeast of Vancouver, Helga Rose derived all her satisfaction in life from two seemingly contradictory habits: the pensioner loved to dress well and to drink Molson's Canadian beer. The widow hated living alone, and she had been delighted when, seven or eight years previously, Ray Boswell, her junior by nearly twenty years, happened along and began to share her small house. Boswell worked occasionally, but mostly the two shared rounds of beer at the local legion.

Helga's friends had long since given up trying to talk to her about the dangers of the life she led. After all, associating with a beer-drinking crowd was probably no harder on a seventy-two-year-old woman than the beer itself would be.

The town collectively assessed, "She'll come to no good," and left it at that.

In Courtenay on Vancouver Island, Jaime James (also known as Jaime Cochrane, Myfanwy Cochrane, and Myfanwy deRoche), her twelve-year-old daughter, Fern, and their new friend, Bruce Robbins, a man closer to Fern's age than Jaime's, were fed up. Jaime James, especially, was ready to pack it in and start life somewhere else where they'd have a better crack at things.

David Shearing, a man in his early twenties, lived with his mother near Clearwater, B.C. Maintaining any sort of equilibrium had always been a struggle: he was a loner who lacked the social skills necessary for the easy interactions he observed and envied in his schoolmates. Even the most ordinary day-to-day situations were a challenge for David, and now life seemed to be conspiring to throw even more at him.

Each small success he experienced seemed to be followed by a substantial set back. In 1980, after earning a second-class, heavy duty mechanics' ticket, Shearing moved to Wainwright, Alberta. While working there as a truck driver he met and began to date a young woman. Never what anyone would term a "ladies' man," Shearing was delighted when a romance blossomed. She was a local girl and, apparently, as smitten with David Shearing as he was with her. Only months after their first date his girlfriend was killed in a car accident. Badly shaken, he'd moved back to Clearwater.

Later the same year there had been another fatal car accident. This time he had been directly involved. Shearing had been to a party and, really, the evening hadn't gone too badly. He'd enjoyed himself and had felt flattered when a couple of people who'd had too much to drink asked him for a lift home.

While driving on the country road he had turned a corner and had immediately come upon a body sprawled across the road. He had no chance to stop and ran over the prone figure. Terrified, he and his friends fled the scene leaving the now dead body unattended and the accident unreported. Eventually the police caught up with him, but after an investigation, authorities placed the bulk of the blame for the accident on the victim, who was drunk and had passed out in the middle of the road. Police did not lay charges.

Then, less than two years later, David Shearing's father died unexpectedly. The man's death apparently pulled the last pin out from David's stability. Either he was no longer interested in keeping up the pretense of a normal existence or he no longer had the capability. David began to drink heavily and often.

George and Edith Johnson registered with the gatekeepers at Wells Gray Provincial Park on August 3, 1982. They happily set up camp and filled the next few days easily while waiting for Jackie, Bob, Karen, and Janet to join them.

A labour dispute between the British Columbia government and its employees meant that the day the couple checked into the park was the last day for some weeks that park employees were on the job. This didn't bother the Bentleys at all. They were completely self-sufficient. They explored the woods, bathed in the nearby streams, read and rested until the exciting moment, later in the week, when they drove back out to the park gate to meet the Johnsons and guide them to the campsite they'd chosen.

The little girls and the grandparents greeted each other with equal enthusiasm. Bob and Jackie Johnson, too, were sincerely glad to see Jackie's parents, especially to see them looking so well rested and healthy.

Camping in Wells Gray Provincial Park required considerably more expertise than staying at a privately owned campground that offered cement parking pads, hot showers, laundry facilities, power hook-ups, and heated swimming pools. This was the wilderness and it required real camping skills. Visitors had to bring the resources they needed or do without.

As the park is home to wild animals, one of the resources wary campers must carry is a rifle. The Bentleys and the Johnsons knew this; and the day the six met they had at least two. They kept a weapon nearby while they enjoyed one another's company around their first evening's campfire together. Not long after dark, Karen and Janet, exhausted from the long day's drive and all the excitement, curled up in their sleeping bags. The adults weren't far behind. The Johnsons' tent was beside their daughters' and only metres away from the Bentleys' camper.

Unaware of being spied on, the adults wished one another good nights and turned in, happily anticipating their first full day together in a very long time. How many days the six could spend together was determined by Bob's job — Gorman Brothers Lumber Mill expected their chief sawyer back on the job Monday, August 16.

David Shearing had developed insomnia. To fill in the long, sleepless nights he'd taken to wandering the back roads of south central British Columbia. He knew the area well, having been born and raised there. On Friday, August 6, 1982, he spotted the Bentleys and the Johnsons early in the evening. Irresistibly drawn to the evident joy and rapport the six relatives exhibited, David Shearing lurked around their campsite, undetected, throughout the night.

When the day came that "Bobbie," as many at the lumber mill called him, did not turn up for work, his fellow employees felt concerned. Because of Bob's impeccable work record they presumed, at first, that they'd gotten the dates mixed up and perhaps they were expecting him too soon. By Wednesday a fellow sawyer decided to check with Bob's neighbours. Maybe someone had seen them or at least knew something. But inquiries turned up nothing, and the worry intensified.

On Sunday, August 22, Jerry Ambrozuk rented a Cessna 150 from Sol Air Aviation, in Richmond, B.C. The firm knew and trusted the young man: he'd taken his pilot training there the previous year and had since taken more specialized lessons in the procedures necessary to fly in mountain areas. So, that day, accompanied by his high-school sweetheart, Diane Babcock, Jerry registered a flight plan to Vancouver. The trip was less than twenty-five nautical miles, which meant that an emergency locator transmitter wasn't required.

The people renting the plane to Ambrozuk had no reason to suspect his plans were anything other than what he indicated. It seemed entirely appropriate that the young man would want to log a few hours flying time while enjoying the company of his girlfriend.

Later, Diane called her parents in nearby Burnaby to let them know she'd arrived safely in Penticton.

"We're going to spend the day at the beach," she added. Her parents found nothing out of the ordinary in the call. Although, like most teenage girls, Diane had struggled to gain independence from her parents at a more rapid rate than they were comfortable with, most of that seemed to be behind them.

Diane had done well in school socially, athletically and academically. Now, they believed, she was serious about the psychiatric nursing program she was taking at the British Columbia Institute of Technology. The future looked bright for the eighteen year old, and her parents were both proud and even a bit relieved at how well things appeared to be working out.

They liked young Jerry. He was an extrovert who apparently had firm plans for his future and, although the two had never mentioned marriage, their relationship was obviously serious.

Kurt Krack loved the interior of British Columbia and he knew portions of Wells Gray Provincial Park well. On his days off from his job as a butcher, he frequently hiked the park trails. In season he'd pick huckleberries while enjoying the natural beauty of the surroundings. On Sunday, August 22, while on just such a berry picking expedition, he noticed something in the park that didn't belong there and that he had never noticed before. It appeared to be the burned-out shell of a car. Krack thought little of his sighting. He presumed thieves had stripped and burned a car to destroy evidence. He finished his picking and left the park.

The next day, Monday, August 23, Bob Johnson was fully a week overdue. The company's owners contacted some of the Johnson's relatives. No one had heard from the family or, for that matter, from Jackie's parents, George and Edith Bentley. Feeling something was dreadfully wrong, those concerned filed a missing persons report with the RCMP.

Frustratingly, there was little the police could do. Yes, the families were missing but on that information alone how could you conduct a search? No one even knew for sure whether the six had actually met as they intended to. Park records confirmed that the older couple checked into the campground on August 3, but, after that, the labour dispute meant there was no one in the park to keep records.

By now newspapers began carrying reports of the missing families. Police asked anyone who might have information to come forward. Kurt Krack wondered whether the presumably stolen and definitely torched vehicle he'd spotted some days ago might be connected in any way to the search for the missing campers. Krack called the Abbottsford detachment of the RCMP. The response he received surprised and considerably annoyed him: his call was virtually dismissed out of hand with a brief, "That's not our area, sir. You'll have to contact the Clearwater detachment."

Knowing the second call would be long distance, and by now wondering about the importance of his information, Kurt Krack let the matter drop.

On Monday, August 30, the RCMP, civilians, volunteers, relatives and friends joined forces to search for answers in the Bentley/Johnson disappearance. The massive effort went unrewarded.

Most people in western Canada were, by now, aware that six people, ranging in age from eleven to sixty-six and all related by blood or marriage, had apparently disappeared without a trace.

For the Ambrozuk and the Babcock families, the reports they heard and read were of considerably less importance than the fact that their own children had not been seen in over a week — not since Jerry rented the plane and flew, with Diane, to Penticton.

On the same Monday that so many B.C. residents were helping police comb the rugged wilderness of Wells Gray Provincial Park, Jerry Ambrozuk phoned a longtime friend.

When Tom Pawlowski answered the call, he recognized his friend's voice immediately.

"I'm in New York," the missing man said.

"Yeah, right, sure you are, Jerry. Where are you really and what have you done? You've got everyone here pretty worried and upset, you know. I think you should call your parents and Diane's too, for that matter."

"Okay, okay, so I'm not in New York. I'm in some dump of a town down here."

With that, Ambrozuk disconnected the call, leaving Tom even more puzzled than before. After taking time to compose himself, Pawlowski phoned Jerry Ambrozuk's father, Ted.

As Tom and Ted suspected he might, Jerry Ambrozuk called Tom a few days later. This time the call didn't take Tom completely by surprise, and Jerry's father was there with him.

"Look," the teenage pilot began. "We had all this planned. I crashed the plane. It's in Bitterroot Lake near White ... [transmission garbled]. Diane's dead. I couldn't get her out of her safety harness. I swam to shore and now I'm on the run. You'll never see me again."

"Where are you?" Pawlowski asked.

"Never mind that. You won't find me. We've had all this planned, but Diane wasn't supposed to die. I wanted to get away from everything, and then a few days before I was ready to go she said she wanted to come too."

"Jerry, your father's here with me. He'd like to talk to you."

Hearing the distinctive click of a receiver being placed back on the cradle, Tom Pawlowski knew his calls of "Jerry, Jerry" were futile.

Moments later the two called police.

On Monday, September 13, Kurt Krack happened to be chatting with a friend — a police officer from Chilliwack. He told the other man of his sighting the previous month, and complained about the reception he got when he tried to report the location of the burned out vehicle to the Abbottsford RCMP.

Krack's friend immediately assessed the importance of what his friend was saying and he contacted his superiors. An RCMP cruiser soon arrived at Kurt Krack's door. Worrying whether he'd inadvertently caused a lot of commotion for nothing, Krack got into the cruiser and directed the officer to the entrance of the Wells Gray Park. The officer driving Krack radioed ahead, and half a dozen additional police officers met them at the park gate. From there, the entourage, led by the rather overwhelmed civilian, proceeded into the forest.

Krack walked straight to the edge of a bluff and pointed directly down below. There, without question, lay the burned out shell of a car.

Police officers approached the wreckage with a sinking realization that they would soon know the answer to the mystery of what had become of the Bentleys and the Johnsons. They cordoned off the area and posted a guard for the night while they assembled the experts needed to investigate the find. Four adults' bodies were in the back seat. The remains of two smaller skeletons were in the car's trunk.

The next day, while some officers scoured the ground around the remains of the car, others delicately placed bone fragments, charred flesh and the odd wisps of hair from the six bodies into plastic bags. These gruesome tasks completed, a crane moved into place and lifted what had been Bob Johnson's 1979 Dodge Caravelle onto a flatbed truck.

The police officers whom Tom Pawlowski and Ted Ambrozuk contacted noted the information and also passed it on to Canadian aviation authorities who then contacted authorities in Flathead County, Montana. Jerry's references to Bitterroot Lake and "White" had narrowed the search to this state.

Shortly after receiving the information, police, there, began a sonar scan search of Little Bitterroot Lake near Whitefish. All the activity attracted the attention of local residents who came forward with additional information.

"I saw a guy camping here a couple of days ago," one informant told the American officials. When shown a photograph of Jaroslaw Ambrozuk, the man confirmed that it was indeed the man he'd seen camping at the side of the lake. "He was soaking wet but the duffel bag that sat beside him was dry. I can show you where he was when I saw him."

Not far from Ambrozuk's abandoned campsite, police found a green plastic garbage bag. The bag had been taped to strengthen and waterproof it. A rope was attached to the bag, presumably to make it easier to tow while swimming to shore. This, investigators reasoned, accounted for the fact the duffel bag was dry while the man was wet.

"I found this," another informant offered, handing the charred remains of an aircraft radio over to police. It matched the type that would have been aboard the Cessna 150.

On Tuesday, September 14, 1982, at her home in Hope, B.C., Helga Rose's party days came to an abrupt and violent end. Someone stabbed Helga and her longtime companion, Ray Boswell, to death.

On Wednesday, September 15, RCMP received a report of a burned out camper/pickup being found roughly two hundred kilometres north of Wells Gray Provincial Park. RCMP in Prince George immediately tracked down the vehicle, but it did not meet the description of the Bentley's truck.

With ample justification, British Columbia's residents became concerned. Rocked just years before by Clifford Olson's horrendous deeds, an atmosphere approaching alarm gripped the population. Newspapers carried reviews of unsolved mass murders in the province's history. A generalized personality profile gave readers an idea of the type of person who might have committed one or more of these crimes.

Predictably, rumours ran rampant: that the Bentleys and the Johnsons had gone for a hike and upon returning had disturbed thieves who then killed them; that the murderers ambushed the family because they needed the camper and camping equipment to make a safe getaway from previous crimes; and that the Bentleys and the Johnsons had inadvertently stumbled onto a valuable and, of course, illegal crop of marijuana. These stories somehow made the situation easier to bear — at least they were theories, which was all anyone else had about any of the recent murders and disappearances.

Jaime James, her daughter, Fern, and their travelling companion, Bruce Robbins, had not been seen since they were involved in a car accident in Prince George on September 4. Concern for their well-being mounted after police found some of Jaime's letters and clothing, her unemployment insurance cheques, her purse, and a .22 calibre rifle near the site of a campfire pit in an isolated area.

Jaime's mother told police she had no idea where the trio might be. Checking with her former workmates in Courtenay revealed that when she left that town Jaime James had made it clear she hoped never to return.

The RCMP assembled a variety of experts in the Bentley/Johnson case: dentists, chemists, anthropologists, and even physicists to try to identify the charred remains found in the park. In the end, all the experts could really do was offer educated guesses. Few doubted that the remains found in the burned out car were once the bodies of Edith and George Bentley, their daughter, Jackie, her husband, Bob, and their two daughters.

Who murdered them and how remained a complete mystery. The solution, authorities thought, lay in finding the Bentleys camper, which was widely presumed to have been used as a getaway vehicle.

Meanwhile, Jerry Ambrozuk's calls to his friend Tom continued. Jerry expressed annoyance that searchers hadn't yet found the plane containing Diane Babcock's body. In two further calls, he gave detailed directions to the wreck. Telephone company records showed that the second call originated from Dallas, Texas, while the third and final call came from from a bus depot in New York City.

Ambrozuk, of course, wasn't the only one feeling frustrated that the plane hadn't been found. The bottom of the glacially created lake was silt, so searchers had to contend with poor visibility. It finally took both sonar probes and remote camera equipment to locate the wreck nearly eighty metres below the icy surface of the lake. Once searchers found the plane's resting spot, the Flathead County Sheriff's Department lost no time in bringing it to the shore.

Tragically, Diane Babcock's body, still partially strapped in, as Ambrozuk had explained in his telephone call, sat in the passenger's seat.

In the town of Hope, a fairly straightforward police investigation had led to the arrest of the man they believed to be guilty of murdering Helga Rose and Ray Boswell. The murder weapon remained at the scene, so solving the murder proved to be merely a matter of putting the pieces of the puzzle together.

Jaime James, Bruce Robbins, and little Fern James reappeared as suddenly as they'd disappeared. The commotion surrounding their travels took them completely by surprise. The three apparently found the authorities' actions as confusing as the authorities found theirs. But the trio's re-appearance at least accounted for some of those whom B.C. residents feared might have come to a violent end.

Police shipped the burned shell that was once the Johnson's family car to a lab in Vancouver. Investigators had little to go on even having found the car. Whoever set fire to it had chosen a highly effective fire accelerant. If the murderer or murderers had left any clues in the vehicle, the ragingly hot fire had destroyed them.

Every detail turned up in this horrific mass murder was shared with police departments across the United States and Canada. Personality profiles showed that people capable of committing mass murders tended to be primitive in their behaviour patterns — incapable of determining alternative methods of resolving conflicts or obtaining pleasure. Their behaviour often showed little more sophistication than that of prehistoric man. Everyone involved hoped that by sharing information with other police departments the RCMP might determine that the Bentleys' and Johnsons' killers were already in jail somewhere else.

Despite their best hopes and efforts, the police remained frustrated. To add to their discomfort, they were receiving bad press about their handling of the case. From Allan Williams, the provincial Attorney General, down to Clearwater friends and neighbours of the deceased, people criticized the police procedure that had delayed Kurt Krack's lead being acted on. This action, people believed, had bought the killer or killers a ten-day head start.

Most people in and around Clearwater consoled each other with the hope that the vicious murderers had stolen the Bentley's truck and were now as far away from the murder site as they could possibly get. Police investigation around the area helped to confirm that notion. Shortly after finding the bodies, police had interviewed nearby residents, including David Shearing, and had asked them if they recalled any unusual activity in early August. No one did.

And so the winter of 1982-83 approached rapidly with no progress in solving the horrific mass murder of the previous summer. The only hope for justice in the apparently motiveless and senseless slaughter of six innocent family members lay in finding the Bentley's missing camper. Throughout the winter, police received reports of sightings of the vehicle. Often the eye witnesses included detailed descriptions of two male occupants. Police artists drew composite sketches and with each new report refined the likenesses.

On September 28, police on Vancouver Island stopped what they presumed was the Bentley's camper. Consistent with the many scattered reports they found two French-Canadian men driving the rig. Although similar, it wasn't the Bentley's truck, and the two men had no trouble proving their innocence.

Unfailingly, crimes that attract the attentions of the press and the public also spark the interest of those who live on the periphery of reality. Some of these people become well known to certain police services, and investigators have come to expect to hear from them under the right circumstances.

The Bentley/Johnson murders were no exception. Strange information poured in and, of course, every lead, no matter how bizarre, received follow-up action. Any one of these "reports" might contain a nugget of truth which could lead authorities to the killers.

Because they weren't ready to dismiss anything out of hand, the police always felt frustrated when they received anonymous communications. Sometimes people wrote long detailed letters to the police but left them unsigned and with no return address. Other people contacted radio stations giving detailed scenarios that they "knew" to be true, but refused to leave their names.

Although the sorts of people who leave these leads rarely function effectively in society, they are often very aware of events around them. This means that the information they offer can tie in amazingly, and confusingly, well with actual events. For instance, the Clearwater RCMP detachment received an untraceable letter from a person claiming psychic powers. He or she stated that two men murdered the six and stole the camper. Shortly after the murders, these men had broken into a local cafe.

Because of the magnitude of the crime, police were accepting the possibility that more than one person was involved. Also, because the camper still hadn't been found, many people accepted the premise that the murderer had stolen it. To complicate matters, there had been a break-in at a Clearwater cafe shortly after police had located the Johnson's car and its appalling cargo.

Even an unnamed, retired RCMP officer offered his experienced opinion by telling a reporter with the *Toronto Star* that the families had been killed by psychotic teenagers.[1]

With standard investigation procedures proving ineffective, police knew they'd have to take new approaches. And so, in the early spring of 1983, two RCMP officers from Kamloops detachment, Corporal Laurie DeWitt and Constable Gerry Dalen, went to work assembling a camper-pick-up truck exactly duplicating the Bentley's missing rig.

On May 9, the two, driving the twin vehicle, left Kamloops and headed east. A large sign on the back of the camper detailed who they were and why they were on the road. Everyone hoped that this set-up would attract attention and possibly jog someone's memory about something they might have seen but never thought to mention. Police badly needed to find someone who could point them in a new direction — the direction of the murderer who had so far eluded them.

The replica did attract the intended attention as it made its way across the prairies, following what investigators deduced was the fugitives' route, but unfortunately, either potential witnesses didn't remember anything or, if they did, they weren't offering statements.

However, Officers DeWitt and Dalen remained optimistic. Both held to the belief that the solution lay in northwestern Quebec. This is where they began to hear the sorts of reports for which the journey was intended.

"Yes, I saw them. Two men driving an outfit just like this one."

"I saw them. The one had eyes that just bored right through you."

Others saw similarities between descriptions of the supposed occupants and convicted rapists in northern mining towns. Assembling the replica had been expensive, and the journey was time-consuming, but by mid-May 1983, it looked as though it might lead police to the solution they sought.

But despite all the promising leads and raised hopes, by the end of May the two RCMP officers had reversed their route across roughly two-thirds of the country. They arrived back in Kamloops no wiser than when they had left.

And life in and around the murder site and the town of Clearwater started to return to normal. People's lives, once again, began to centre on events other than the murders. Some lives, of course, were irreparably damaged; others continued on, more or less unaffected. David Shearing, for instance, felt secure enough to move from his mother's Clearwater home to Tumbler Ridge, four hundred kilometres north, near Dawson Creek.

By September 1983, Jerry Ambrozuk still hadn't been found despite being wanted by police in the United States on a charge of negligent homicide. (The equivalent Canadian term is manslaughter.)

Korky Derby of the Sheriff's Office in Flathead County, Montana, stated that she felt Ambrozuk was receiving help in order to remain undetected, despite the best efforts of the police.

In Canada the RCMP hired additional personnel to cope with the leads still coming in about the Bentley/Johnson murders. Infra-red scanning equipment proved that the Bentley's camper was no longer in the provincial park. Police surmised that the killers had escaped in the camper and headed to eastern Canada. And they initiated a massive mail-out campaign to anyone who had registered at the park the previous summer. They also circulated a police artist's sketches of what the wanted men might look like. A made-for-television docudrama re-enacted, for all of Canada, how the murders might have taken place. Still no substantial leads showed up — until Tuesday, October 19, 1983, when a new report regarding the park murders shocked all but a very few people.

Provincial forestry workers Doug Kehler and Peter Miller had strayed only slightly off the path of an old logging road. They were attempting to determine the amount of damage done to soil in the area during a recent forest fire. There, in front of them, badly burned and effectively hidden in the dense bush, lay what they knew, almost instantly, to be the camper that police had been searching for.

Noting the barely visible licence number, the two forgot their soil study and ran to contact the RCMP. Within minutes a crowd of uniformed men joined the two who'd phoned them. All the leads regarding a killer or killers loose somewhere in eastern Canada evaporated as they stared at what was once an expensively equipped 1981 Ford truck. For, there it sat, a mere two kilometres from the murder site. Did this mean the killer remained nearby as well?

One of the few people not surprised by the discovery was Bill Mattenley, who had co-ordinated the original search. He explained that the bush in that area was dense enough to camouflage the truck. Another unsurprised person was a retired police officer from Edmonton who had asserted all along that the camper had never left the park. The third unsurprised person was a worried, former-Clearwater resident.

Police activity surrounding the case had slowed considerably over the past months as leads dried up, but this discovery changed all that. A Sikorsky S-61 helicopter flew into the park to remove the camper from its resting place of fourteen months. Basic police work started up again. RCMP officers once more conducted door-to-door interviews with residents in the Clearwater area. The residents, frightened at the possibility of a mass murderer in their midst, were grateful to see uniformed investigators at work in their community. Everyone questioned tried to answer the officers' questions as fully as possible, no matter how long the interview.

"Has anyone spoken to you in the past fourteen months about buying or selling a pickup truck or a camper attachment or any camping equipment?" the police routinely asked.

"You know, now that you mention it, I do seem to recall something like that last year, maybe late summer or early fall. This guy asked me about registering a camper. I got the idea more from what he didn't say than from what he did say that it was hot," a resident told a police officer during an interview in Clearwater. "I think he was also concerned about a bullet hole in one of the doors."

That last sentence sparked an intense reaction in the young officer. Barely able to control his voice, he probed further.

"Do you remember who it was you had this discussion with?"

"Oh, yes, of course I do. I've known him since he was a kid."

Offering only cursory thanks, the officer hurried to the police station. He needed to talk to his boss. Police had purposely not released all of the data they'd amassed in examining the camper. No one outside the force, unless he was the killer, should have known there was a bullet hole in the door of the Bentley's camper.

Before the end of the day, several high-ranking RCMP officers re-interviewed that same Clearwater resident. Shortly after, they reconvened in their offices to map out an arrest strategy. At all costs they must prevent alerting the suspect.

And so it was that on Saturday, November 19, 1983, several Kamploops RCMP members travelled north. They had no trouble locating Shearing in the small community of Tumbler Ridge.

"We just need to talk to you a bit about that hit and run you were involved in a couple of years ago," the officers informed the startled David Shearing. He went with them willingly.

After reviewing the facts of the 1980 accident, an RCMP Inspector then commented in what he hoped sounded like an off-hand manner that finding the Bentley's camper had certainly been a surprise.

The seasoned police officers watched as David William Shearing's body tensed noticeably. The atmosphere in the interrogation room changed perceptibly. Ten hours later, the interrogation ended — and the Mounties knew they had their man.

On Monday, November 21, 1983, shackled, handcuffed and heavily guarded, David Shearing, now twenty-four years old, appeared in Kamloops' old provincial courthouse. Despite the fact police had released only a brief statement, spectators packed the courtroom. People could hardly believe the mass murderer had been one of their neighbours. Some had graduated with Shearing from the high school in Clearwater only five years before. Shearing's relatives expressed shock bordering on disbelief.

Even David Shearing himself was startled when he saw the crowded courtroom. He held his head low and cast his eyes to the floor as he listened to the charges against him. With each charge, his six-foot, two-hundred-pound frame shrank.

Following his initial confrontation with the RCMP, Shearing began to show relief. He willingly confessed to the crimes, explaining two and sometimes three times just exactly how he'd carried out each part of his grisly deeds.

Under heavy police escort Shearing re-visited the scene of the crimes and re-enacted portions of the events for the officers. He pointed to where the families had been camped and where he'd hidden while observing them. A police photographer filmed Shearing's explanation as evidence.

It seemed to be important to Shearing that authorities understand the details of each move he had made.

"I hadn't expected to see anyone camping so it surprised me. I hid and just watched them the first evening. I was going to stay all night but I moved and I think they heard me. They started to look toward where I was hiding so I left and went home. The next afternoon I went back to see if they were still there. They were. I watched them for a little while longer, I don't really know how long. The kids went to bed in their tent. The others sat around a campfire. I hid behind their camper until I had the four adults in easy range. Then I just shot them and went to the tent and shot the two girls."

What was his motive? Why had he coldly approached six completely innocent, productive, happy, and defenseless human beings and stolen their lives?

"I don't know," Shearing answered consistently.

"After I killed them I drank some beer. Then I carried the bodies and put them in the car, the kids in the trunk. Then I left."

It was several days later, Shearing explained, that he drove the car, with the bodies still in it, to the spot Kurt Krack had happened upon while gathering huckleberries.

Shearing had dosed the car with gasoline, lit it on fire, and watched the flames destroy most of the evidence of his unspeakable crime.

Shearing had returned to the crime scene again the next night. After stealing a few pieces of camping equipment from the camper, he drove it to a spot just behind the burned out car. He left the camper there that night.

Form 2 PCR CONAIRM. 6/80)

CANADA
PROVINCE OF BRITISH COLUMBIA **INFORMATION**

Prov._____
Sup._____
Cty. _____

This is the information of Sqt. M.W.C. EASTHAM, a member of the Royal Canadian Mounted Police, acting on behalf of Her Majesty the Queen, of the City of Kamloops, Province of British Columbia, (the "informant")

The informant says that he has reasonable and probable grounds to believe and does believe that

Count #1:

David William SHEARING, between the 6th day of August, A.D. 1982, and the 13th day of August, A.D. 1982, inclusive, at or near Clearwater, in the Province of British Columbia, did commit second degree murder on the person of Edith BENTLEY, contrary to Section 218 of the Criminal Code of Canada.

Count #2:

David William SHEARING, between the 6th day of August, A.D. 1982, and the 13th day of August, A.D. 1982, inclusive, at or near Clearwater, in the Province of British Columbia, did commit second degree murder on the person of George Edward BENTLEY, contrary to Section 218 of the Criminal Code of Canada.

Count #3:

David William SHEARING, between the 6th day of August, A.D. 1982, and the 13th day of August, A.D. 1982, inclusive, at or near Clearweater, in the Province of British Columbia, did commit second degree murder on the person of Robert Clarence JOHNSON, contrary to Section 218 of the Criminal Code of Canada.

Count #4:

David William SHEARING, between the 6th day of August, A.D. 1982, and the 13th day of August, A.D. 1982, inclusive, at or near Clearwater, in the Province of British Columbia, did commit second first degree murder on the person of Jacqueline Louise JOHNSON, contrary to Section 218 of the Criminal Code of Canada.

Count #5:

David William SHEARING, between the 6th day of August, A.D. 1982, and the 13th day of August, A.D. 1982, inclusive, at or near Clearwater, in the Province of British Columbia, did commit second degree murder on the person of Janet Lee JOHNSON, contrary to Section 218 of the Criminal Code of Canada.

Count #6:

David William SHEARING, between the 6th day of August, A.D. 1982, and the 13th day of August, A.D. 1982, inclusive, at or near Clearwater, in the Province of British Columbia, did commit second degree murder on the person of Karen Louise JOHNSON, contrary to Section 218 of the Criminal Code of Canada.

SWORN Before me this

_____DAY OF November___1983__

_____
(SIGNATURE OF INFORMANT)

AT THE CITY OF KAMLOOPS
        BRITISH COLUMBIA

_____
                CONFIRMED

_____
A JUSTICE OF THE PEACE FOR THE
PROVINCE OF BRITISH COLUMBIA

_____
A JUSTICE OF THE PEACE FOR THE
PROVINCE OF BRITISH COLUMBIA

Government of British Columbia's charge sheet against David Shearing.

"I thought about keeping the camper. It was a good rig," the murderer explained.

Apparently deciding the risk outweighed the benefits, David Shearing had returned to foul the pristine beauty of Wells Gray Park once again. He drove the Bentley's camper, this time to the spot where it had remained hidden for more than a year. And repeating the steps he had taken to destroy the Johnson's car, David Shearing set the camper on fire.

Kamloops lawyer Fred Kaatz took on the responsibility of defending the self-confessed murderer's rights in court. Shearing waived his right to a preliminary hearing, and his trial, the last major case ever tried in the historic Kamloops courthouse, was scheduled to begin Monday, April 16, 1984.

During the Christmas between Shearing's arrest and trial, Tom Pawlowski found an unexpected card in his mailbox: Jerry Ambrozuk sent him season's greetings, and the card bore a Dallas, Texas, postmark.

There were few surprises at David Shearing's trial. In a highly emotional state the man pleaded guilty to six charges of second-degree murder. Because there was no evidence that Shearing had planned the killings, the charge wasn't first-degree murder.

Supreme Court Justice Harry McKay assigned the maximum punishment available under Canadian law. David William Shearing would serve a twenty-five-year sentence, without possibility of parole.

And so, although justice had been done, perhaps the largest question concerning the crime remained unanswered.

What was Shearing's motive?

None was ever spoken.

The press carried comments from RCMP officers involved in the case that the file would never be completely closed until a motive for the killings had been determined.

David Shearing began serving his sentence alongside other murderers at Kent Institution in Agassiz, just outside Vancouver.

Rumours of a possible motive surfaced here and there occasionally over the next few months. Then, in January 1986, the rumours became news stories on the front pages of Canadian daily newspapers. RCMP reportedly informed relatives of the Bentleys and the Johnsons that Shearing had sexually molested at least some of the victims over a period of days after first encountering them.

When the story broke, both the RCMP and Shearing's lawyer, Fred Kaatz, refused comment. Bob Hunter, who'd acted as Crown counsel during the trial, scoffed at the possibility, saying that such a scenario was impossible as

Shearing had left the murder site each day to return home and go to work. This would have allowed more than ample opportunity for the family to escape, he reasoned.

In the end, Linda Bentley, Edith and George Bentley's daughter-in-law, reminded the press that only one person knew exactly what had occurred early in August 1982, in Wells Gray Provincial Park. And why would anyone take such a man's word for anything?

At this writing, the Flathead County Sheriff's office in Kalispell, Montana, reports that Jaroslaw Ambrozuk is still at large.

"We have an active warrant on him," they confirm.[2] And the events connected with Jerry's and Diane's flight, her death, and his subsequent travels remain as mysterious as his motives.

THE DEADLY DOCTOR

Doctor. How our society loves that title. The cliché for the ultimately proud parent is, "My son the doctor": the epithet shows up with a frequency unmatched by P. Eng. or LLB; and people often use "doctor" to get reservations and other preferential treatment.

Joseph Antoine Leo Real Bertrand, born July 13, 1913, on his parents' farm near the Quebec/Ontario border, adopted the title "doctor" but Leo Bertrand never saw the inside of a university. It's unlikely that any of the Bertrand children received much of an education. Leo did, however, develop a personality that was mannerly to the point of being officious, and he had an obsession with being stylishly dressed.

In February of 1934, at age 21, the smartly turned out Leo married the comely young Rose Anna Asseline from the neighbouring village of St. Justine de Newton, and the newlyweds moved to Ottawa to begin their life together. For five months they rented a room from an uncle of Leo's, and as soon as they had a bit of money set aside they found a small apartment of their own.

Times were tough. The Great Depression that raged worldwide meant economic hardship for all but the most fortunate. Leo earned a meager living for the two of them as a cab driver. As often happens, Rose became pregnant almost immediately.

The couple made friends with a few of the neighbours in the surrounding flats, and one of those friends was Eugene Picard, a life insurance salesman. When he heard about the forthcoming blessed event, Eugene approached Leo about buying a policy to cover Rose.

"Now that there's a child on the way, you have additional responsibilities," the salesman explained. "What if something happened, God forbid, to Rose? How would you look after your new baby? You need some insurance, life insurance on Rose Anna. Everyone has it. It would give you the money you'd need to hire someone to take care of the baby if Rose was taken from you."

"You're a dreamer, Picard. I can barely pay my rent and buy groceries. I haven't even bought a new tie since we were married; I certainly don't have money for insurance."

"You'd be surprised. I can set it up so you'd only pay a little bit each week. A smart man like you will find the money to pay for something this important. Give me less than a dollar a week and I'll fix it so you'll have $5,000 insurance on Rose's life — and double indemnity."

"I don't know what that means, and I don't have an extra dollar a week or even a month."

"The company I work for would give you $5,000 cash if anything should happen to your Rose, and double indemnity would give you twice that if she were to be killed in some sort of an accident," the salesman clarified for his potential client.

"Some company will give me money if Rose dies?" Bertrand questioned incredulously.

"Ten thousand dollars if she dies in an accident," Picard reiterated.

Leo looked baffled, but Picard continued his sales pitch.

"I know it sounds like a lot, Leo, but believe me you'd need that much at least to look after your baby. You'd need to hire someone right away and that's not cheap. You couldn't stay home with the child. You don't know the first thing about looking after an infant and, besides, you'd still need to earn a living."

As an experienced salesman, Eugene Picard could sense that he was overcoming the man's natural resistance to spending money on such an intangible thing as life insurance. He could see the changing expression on his friend's face; Picard knew he was making progress toward a sale.

"Ask anyone, Leo. Insurance is important to young parents," he added, but Leo didn't seem to hear him. Not knowing what else to do, Picard launched into the "closing" he'd learned in sales classes.

"Leave it to me, Leo. I'll make all the arrangements and have my company draw up the policy. You won't have to pay anything until I deliver the documents. That'll give you time to set aside enough for the first payment."

"How soon can you do this?" Leo probed.

"If it's the payment you're worried about, I can postpone that for almost a week."

"No, no. I'd like you to do this quickly Eugene. You're right. Life insurance on Rose is very important," Leo concurred, displaying a sudden change of heart. "I've got a few dollars put away. I can give you the first payment right now."

Pleased that he'd enlightened yet another of his friends to what he considered the very sophisticated world of life insurance, Eugene Picard laughed heartily and assured Leo Bertrand that his policy would arrive within a few days.

"You know, Leo, I've always known you were a cut above the rest. It's not everyone who can grasp the importance of insurance. Congratulations. You just leave everything to me."

Despite his initial hesitation in making the financial commitment, Leo Bertrand sought out his friend Eugene several times over the next several days.

"How's my policy coming?" he would ask, or, "There's not going to be any problem getting this arranged, is there?" until the Wednesday, December 19, 1934, when Eugene Picard turned over a $5,000 double indemnity insurance policy to Leo Bertrand. The certificate named Rose Anna Asseline Bertrand as the insured and Joseph Antoine Leo Real Bertrand as the beneficiary. It's not known whether the pregnant young woman knew of the arrangements.

The next day, feeling rather extravagant, Leo Bertrand took the day off work, and he and his now-insured, pregnant wife took a drive in the country to his parents' farm. They enjoyed their visit with the older couple, and when they left to make their way back home to Ottawa, Rose's mother-in-law gave them a large crate of fresh eggs. Leo's parents hadn't been able to help the young people out financially, but the senior Bertrand couple did have a productive chicken farm. This gift would at least assure the elder Mrs. Bertrand that her daughter-in-law would get the extra protein and iron that a pregnant woman required.

It was late in the evening when Leo and Rose left his parents' farm, the crate of eggs sitting snugly between the two on the front seat of their car.

Some days later, a neighbour of the elder Bertrands, Alcide Melthot, reported that he'd seen the couple driving south toward the village of St. Zotique, on the edge of Lac St. Francis.

"I know it was them. I grew up with Leo and I know his car. I was walking on the highway. It was late, nearly midnight. The night was clear and the moon shone brightly, so I wasn't concerned that he wouldn't be able to see me. But it was strange. He kept coming at me until he nearly hit me. I jumped out of the way, and he swerved just at the last minute. Otherwise he'd have struck me," Melthot recalled.

Not far from there, where the road from St. Polycarpe joins the main highway, there's a stop sign. The Bertrands were also spotted there. Joe Cuerrier, who lived near the junction of the two roadways, reported that he saw a car matching the description of Leo Bertrand's pass through the intersection without acknowledging the stop sign. This captured Joe's attention, not only because the driver had run the stop sign but because he'd driven straight through on the secondary road and not turned onto the highway. The St. Polycarpe road ended in a pier jutting out over Lac St. Francis only 160 metres after it crossed the highway.

Unlike Alcide Melthot, Joe Cuerrier didn't recognize either the car or its occupants, and he wondered who would be driving down to the dock at that hour on a winter's night. He watched as the car came to a stop near the end of the jetty. Concerned, he went out to investigate, but by the time he got around the corner of his house and could once again see the pier, the car was no longer in sight. Presuming the driver had realized his error, turned his car around, and taken the main highway, the relieved Melthot gratefully returned to the warmth of his house.

As he reported the news to his wife, there was an urgent knocking at the Melthot's cottage door.

The man opened it to find a frantic-looking Leo Bertrand shouting nearly hysterically that his car had gone over the pier with his dear pregnant (and well-insured) wife still in the vehicle.

"We'll have to get help," Melthot wisely assessed. "There may still be skaters at the rink. It's not far from here at the White House Hotel. There's bound to be people there who can help us."

Running ahead of Melthot, Bertrand reached the hotel first and burst into the beverage room, calling excitedly, "Help, help. Someone has to help me. My car's gone over the pier and my wife is in it."

The owner of a nearby garage, Romeo Avon, responded immediately to the apparently desperate man's plea. He told Bertrand to go to the pier and he'd meet him there with some tools and a block and tackle.

Joe Cuerrier rounded up half a dozen skaters, all willing to do what they could to help. Most of those gathered on the dock were longtime area residents and therefore familiar with both the lake and the dock. They knew that the freezing water, which was just over a metre below the pier and slightly less than three metres deep, could kill.

With help now at hand, Bertrand calmed down enough to explain that the car had balanced on the edge of the jetty for a moment before toppling into the frigid waters. Armed with this information the searchers focused their search directly off the end of the dock.

In retrospect, what didn't seem reasonable was Leo Bertrand's questions to garage owner Romeo Avon about the possible damage that submersion in the icy lake could do to a car. He specifically inquired about the effects on his car's oil, antifreeze, and gasoline. Although caught up by the urgency of the search, Romeo Avon recalled later that, even at the time, the questions seemed strange from a man in Leo Bertrand's situation. Shortly after the fruitless hunt had begun, police officer Jean Desrosiers arrived on the scene. At almost exactly the same time Leo Bertrand slipped away from the crowd. Despite his absence, the crowd worked on through the night. By 5:00 a.m., they located the vehicle fifteen metres out from the end of the dock, and, by hooking a line onto the car's bumper, winched it out of the icy depths. Rose Anna Bertrand sat lifeless in the passenger's seat, the door beside her locked. The driver's door stood open, with only a carton of farm-fresh eggs blocking what could have been Rose's route to safety.

Officer Desrosiers remained at the scene until sunrise. A straight line of tire tracks leading off the end of the dock had caught his eye. About three metres from the water's edge he noted deeply ground tire tracks. It appeared as though someone had attempted to stop or start a car abruptly at that point. He recorded the evidence for his superiors to investigate and assess.

Officers towed the car to a lockup and examined it carefully. They discovered a hole where the inside door handle on the passenger's side should have been. Minutes later a young constable located the part — in a tool box in the car's trunk.

Police called all those who'd volunteered their help the night before into the police station the next day for questioning. They told identical stories. Leo Bertrand had claimed his car had fallen into the water directly in front of the dock. This continued to puzzle authorities as they had located the car some fifteen metres out into the lake.

Investigators became suspicious that Leo Bertrand had driven his car close to the end of the dock, pulled out the hand throttle and jumped clear. Finding the throttle in the open position confirmed their suspicions.

The crate of eggs on her left and the missing door handle on her right meant Rose Bertrand had been trapped in the car as it sped toward the icy black depths of Lac St. Francis.

When police discovered the insurance policy that salesman Eugene Picard had recently sold to Leo Bertrand, they heartily suspected they weren't dealing with an accident, but with a cold-blooded murder.

Three days after what would have been his first Christmas as a married man, police picked up Leo Bertrand for questioning. He calmly explained to Chief Jargaille that he'd become very sleepy while driving back from visiting his parents at their farm. As a result he'd missed the stop sign at the intersection where he should have turned and gone straight across the highway and out onto the pier.

"As soon as I realized what I'd done, I knew I'd have to turn the car around because it wouldn't have been safe to back up all the way to the highway. I was afraid if I tried, I'd drive off the shoulder of the road and into the ditch. I had no idea I was as close as I was to the edge of the dock. As I attempted to turn the car around, the front wheels went off the edge. I jumped out and tried to hold the car, to keep it from going over but I wasn't able to and it fell into the lake at the end of the pier," Bertrand explained calmly.

That a coroner's jury had already termed the death of his wife an accident doubtless gave the young Mr. Bertrand a calming sense of security. Leo's story, however, did not jibe with the hard evidence found at the scene. His version of the incident left several facts unaccounted for. How did the car get to such a great distance from the dock? And how could Bertrand account for the standard-transmission lever being in second gear? And what caused the distinct tire marks some three metres before the end of the dock?

The investigators turned their evidence over to the Attorney-General's people who, in turn, ordered a surprised Leo Bertrand to stand trial for the murder of his pregnant wife.

The Canadian justice system did not work smoothly for Bertrand. His trial, scheduled for September 25, 1935, had to be postponed due to a dispute between the judge, Mr. Justice C. Wilson, and the two defense lawyers. This necessitated scheduling a second trial. It began Monday, December 2, 1935, just less than a year after the "accident."

Oscar Gagnon and Roch Pinard continued to represent Leo Bertrand. Gerald Fauteux, K.C., served as Crown prosecutor, and Mr. Justice Louis Cousineau oversaw the proceedings.

Fauteux maintained that, in order to collect the recently arranged-for life insurance, Bertrand had murdered his young wife. As evidence, Fauteux presented the damning facts found by investigators at the scene. The missing door handle, the positions of both the gearshift lever and hand throttle, and the fact that they had finally located the car more than fifteen metres from the edge of the dock.

Jean Belique, a civil engineer, testifying as an expert witness, explained that the vehicle would have had to have been travelling at sixty-five kilometres an hour to have landed that far out. Mechanic Paul Godin testified that he had, at the request of the Crown, experimented with Bertrand's car and that it had reached that speed in second gear.

Bertrand's future did not look rosy by the time the prosecution had concluded its case.

Now it was the defense's turn, and lawyers Pinard and Gagnon had done their homework. Under their deft hands, the Crown's case began to unravel.

Eugene Picard, who had supplied the life insurance policy covering Rose Bertrand only days before her untimely death, testified first. He explained to the court that it was he who'd urged purchase of the policy, not the defendant. In addition, Picard recalled riding as a passenger in Bertrand's car some time before the accident. The inside door handle on the passenger's side had been missing at that time.

During the four-day trial, Leo Bertrand sat, composed and alert, in the prisoner's box. He exuded an air of confidence, apparently sure he'd leave the court a free man.

In his summation, defense lawyer Oscar Gagnon stressed that if his client had intended to kill his wife he would not have left so much to chance. How could Bertrand have been sure that his wife would be unable to escape from the car? Surely, if he had wanted to murder his wife in this way, he would have been better advised to have knocked her out before piloting the speeding auto to the edge of the dock. The coroner had carefully examined Mrs. Bertrand's body and found no signs of violence.

Justice Cousineau made no attempt to hide his views. He announced: "Bertrand declared on several occasions that his machine was balancing on the edge of the wharf. There was no current in the lake. Putting aside all expert evidence and merely using common sense, do you think it could have gone that far [out into the lake] had it been balanced? Moreover, the car lay in a straight line from the tracks on the pier. If he'd been trying to turn the car it would have landed just off the dock and at an angle to it."

The judge also pointed out that Bertrand's claim of tiredness lacked credibility. Only moments before this catastrophe, he'd been alert enough to swerve and avoid hitting a pedestrian. He also noted Bertrand's strange behaviour on the dock while others worked feverishly to rescue his drowning wife. Justice Cousineau concluded as follows: "Gentlemen, this is either a case of murder or it is an accident. You will have to decide which, to the best of your consciences. If you decide it is murder it will surely be one of the worst crimes in our annals."

At 5:20 on the afternoon of Thursday, December 6, 1935, the jury in the case of *R. versus Joseph Antoine Leo Real Bertrand* retired to a secure room. After three and a half hours of deliberation they returned to the courtroom ready to hand their decision over to Mr. Justice Cousineau and his court.

"Have you reached a decision?" the judge asked rather rhetorically.

"We have Your Honour."

"Please advise the court of this decision."

The foreman of the jury glanced first at Leo Bertrand and then at the judge. The foreman's pinched mouth and uneasy posture revealed his anxiety. His announcement would displease one of the two.

"We find the defendant 'not guilty' of the charges leveled against him," the man declared in a strained voice.

An all-encompassing stillness fell over the courtroom. The decision hung in the air for a second while all those involved assessed the implication of those words. As was fitting, Judge Cousineau broke the silence: "Mr. Bertrand, you are released from custody. The jury has acquitted you of the crime of which you were charged."

The acquittal prompted Bertrand's first display of emotion. He blinked back tears of relief and joy.

Had Leo Bertrand been a different sort of fellow, he might have taken some time to assess all he'd recently been through. His status had changed from being a bachelor living on his parents farm, to newlywed, expectant father, widower, accused murderer, and now a free man with $10,000 owed to him by an insurance company — more transitions than most people deal with in a lifetime, let alone in less than two years. Perhaps if he'd taken a few months to consider his options, the young man's future would have been different. As philosophical reflections rarely guide the decisions of a testosterone-infused twenty-two year old male, Bertrand's next actions were really not a surprise.

Leo Bertrand, or the "Tuxedo Kid" as he preferred being called then, immediately asked his friend Eugene Picard to process the claim against his timely insurance policy. He used a portion of the money to pay his lawyers Oscar Gagnon and Roch Pinard for their skillful defense; a great deal more, however, went to a well-known local tailor. Leo Bertrand looked forward to regaining his reputation as a flamboyant dresser.

While Bertrand knew that some women loved a flashy dresser, he also knew that hailing a cab or riding a streetcar on a date could dampen a girl's lusty thoughts. He needed to retrieve his car. Or did he? Its unfortunate submersion just a year ago had probably ruined it and, besides, the vehicle still sat in the police compound. Bertrand sincerely wished to minimize any further dealings with the boys in blue.

And so Leo Bertrand did what many young men long to do. He purchased a brand-new, high-powered car.

Within weeks Leo Bertrand was broke. However, not being a man to let adversity get in his way, Leo, accompanied by his friend Anatole Letreille, drove to Russell, Ontario, a small town about forty-five kilometers southeast of Ottawa. They planned on visiting the Bank of Nova Scotia located there.

After parking their car in the laneway behind the bank, they entered the institution with the sincere hope it would be able to help them through their temporary financial difficulties. Letreille approached the tellers while Bertrand went directly to the office of branch manager, Charles H. Stewart. Unfortunately, Stewart had overheard the ruckus caused by Anatole Letreille's announcement: "This is a holdup. Stick 'em up." Stewart could also see Letreille enforcing his demands by waving a gun about wildly.

When Bertrand entered Stewart's office to conduct his part of the pair's transactions, the manager greeted him inhospitably with the barrel of a revolver. In those days bank managers were routinely, if ill-advisedly, expected not only to demonstrate above-average administrative abilities but also to protect the bank's funds. While Stewart's organizational skills served his employers well, he was, by no stretch of the imagination, a sharp-shooter.

The presence of an armed bank manager took the well-turned out Tuxedo Kid quite by surprise. Leo fired wildly, narrowly missing the other man's head. Charles Stewart returned the fire, and both bandits fled to the safety of their waiting getaway car, no wealthier than when it had all begun only minutes before.

The badly shaken bank staff called their local Ontario Provincial Police office and an investigation began. Constable Robert Wannell searched the area behind the bank where several people had reported seeing a car with two male occupants parked a short time before the holdup.

Wannell found a few pieces of paper. He presented these to Inspector W.H. Lowery, the officer in charge of the investigation, who determined the scraps were the remains of someone's lottery ticket.

Piecing the fragments together, the two officers read the following clues: "J.H. Leo Bertr ..." showed up on one part; the number five appeared on another; and the words "Dupont Street, Hull," on a third. Armed with this, the officers had little trouble tracking down both the getaway car and Leo Bertrand. They arrested him on June 21, 1936, just five days after the bungled burglary.

Bertrand's accomplice, Anatole Letreille, was picked up shortly after. Records are not clear as to whether Leo "squealed" on his friend or whether the second arrest was merely the result of further clever police work.

What is clear is that the pair made a second trip to small-town Ontario. This time, however, to the town of L'Orignal to be tried before Mr. Justice Chevrier for the attempted holdup.

The October 19, 1936, trial was noteworthy for the presiding judge. Previously, Chevrier had been the Liberal member of parliament for Ottawa East. This was the first time the lawyer/politician had adjudicated a criminal case.

The two accused stood against damning evidence. Even the lottery ticket that Bertrand had purchased while feeling lucky managed to work against him. A handwriting expert testified that the script he examined on a portion of the ticket exactly matched that on the scraps found by Constable Wannell in the laneway. Eye witnesses confirmed that, indeed, the two men in the prisoners' box were the two they'd seen sitting in the car behind the bank moments before the aborted robbery attempt.

A stolen licence plate bearing a partial fingerprint also turned up in the alley. The print belonged to Leo Bertrand. Evidence piled up against Bertrand. Perhaps the Crown might not even have had to produce the next witness to win a guilty verdict.

Apparently Bertrand was not an astute judge of character, for there, on the witness stand and under oath, stood a man he had trusted. While this man had been serving time in the Carleton County jail, the Ontario Provincial Police had brought Bertrand and Letreille to keep him company. The three must have hit it off well because the two newcomers had confided in their cohort.

The betrayed Bertrand listened as his former confidante explained that they had told him that while waiting for the most auspicious moment to enter the bank branch Leo Bertrand had ripped up and thrown away an outdated lottery ticket. Then, according to the retelling, just moments later, Bertrand and Letreille charged into the bank with guns drawn.

Now, for the second time in less than a year, the ever-smartly-attired Leo Bertrand waited while a jury assessed the evidence against him and weighed his fate. This time the Tuxedo Kid was not so fortunate. On Friday, October 23, after only thirty-five minutes' deliberation, the jury returned a verdict of "guilty as charged."

Mr. Justice Chevrier, conscious of his new responsibilities, spoke to the accused about the verdict and the sentencing.

"I want you two to appreciate that your actions could easily have led you to face a much more serious charge, that of murder. Bertrand, the bullet you fired at Charles Stewart's head missed it's target by only six inches. I fear you two are a great danger to our society and for this reason I am sentencing you to the most severe penalty available to me under these circumstances. Anatole Letreille and Leo Bertrand, you will each serve fifteen years in the penitentiary."

Letreille merely blinked in apparent disbelief. Bertrand reacted more dramatically and nearly collapsed.

The natty dresser was trundled off in a paddy wagon to Kingston Penitentiary where he became known, to anyone who cared, as convict number 4346.

Government paperwork records Bertrand listed his occupation as cab driver, reported his average income as thirty dollars a week, claimed one dependent (whose existence is not further explained), declared that he neither smoked nor drank, and signed away his right to appeal either the verdict or the sentence.

Bertrand apparently adapted well to prison routine, or well enough that no newsworthy incidents occurred for the next several years. But early in 1939, overcrowding at Kingston Penitentiary necessitated transfering a number of prisoners to a more westerly federal institution. On February 16, 1939, Leo Bertrand became convict number 3614 at the penitentiary in Prince Albert, Saskatchewan. Fittingly, he chose work in the jail's tailor shop.

To a naive outsider, Leo Bertrand appeared to have turned over a new leaf. Not only did he serve as an acolyte in the jail's Roman Catholic Chapel, but his leisure activities consisted mainly of playing the violin, and he maintained the excessively polite manner that he'd found effective.

He might as well not have bothered because, despite the intervention of the prison chaplain, Father D'Aoust, Bertrand served most of his fifteen-year sentence. On March 9, 1948, eleven years, four months, and eleven days after being incarcerated, Leo Bertrand regained his freedom.

The paperwork that accompanied Bertrand's release described him as being 35, weighing 164 pounds, being five feet, seven inches in height, and having grey eyes, medium dark features, black hair, and no marks or scars. It was this man, then, who made his way back to Ottawa and the only legal job he knew — cab driving.

Borderline poverty, which forty hours a week driving a cab provided, did not offer much appeal to a man who liked to look like a million dollars. So he left that career in favour of an offer from the Ottawa dry-cleaning firm of Lyle Blackwell, located at 830 Campbell Street. Bertrand worked hard to prove himself to his employers, and within two years he had been promoted to plant foreman.

With increased responsibilities came increased wages, which enabled Leo Bertrand not only to dress in his preferred fashion but to pursue a long-standing dream.

During his twelve-year term, the match boxes of his fellow inmates had not gone unnoticed by Leo, although he was a non-smoker. He'd always had a keen interest in psychology and "things mystical," but he recognized that his lack of accreditation in the field severely hampered his ambitions. The credulous Mr. Bertrand found the solution to his dilemma printed on his cellmates' discarded match-book covers.

"Earn your degree by mail," these advertisements urged — an ideal short-cut for a person not much bent on academics. With the wages paid to him at the Blackwell company, Bertrand soon accumulated the required fifty dollars and mailed it to an American college of questionable repute. Within a short time, Leo Bertrand, had become Joseph Antoine Leo Real Bertrand, Doctor of Divinity, Psychology, Philosophy, and even Metaphysics.

Those addressing Leo Bertrand were now reminded, should they have slipped up, that he was not merely Mr. but Dr. One wonders if his mother developed a sudden pride in her ex-convict son. Even if she didn't, other women evidently became suitably impressed. Twenty-one-year-old Ruth Bouchard was one of those. A prim and proper school marm, Ruth insisted that each of her dates with the dashing "Dr." Bertrand be chaperoned, usually by one of her sisters. Leo Bertrand seemed delighted by his new-found relationship with the prudish Miss Bouchard.

About the same time, a new sign appeared in a business district of Ottawa. Leo rented office space and started a private practice offering emotional and psychotherapeutic counselling to the unhappy and unwary. He restricted office hours to evenings because, despite his newly acquired qualifications, Bertrand needed to retain his position at the dry-cleaning firm. He had rent to pay on his small apartment on Lisgar Street and now office rent as well.

In spite of the financial discomfort, Leo Bertrand purchased a used Cadillac.

As foreman at the dry-cleaning plant, his responsibilities included supervision of the seamstresses, one of whom was fifty-three-year-old Marie Blanche Rosa Charette. Her husband had died some four years previously, and she had inherited a modest fortune, by post-war standards. When Marie met Bertrand in 1950, she owned two rooming houses, in addition to valuable personal effects.

A generous and good-hearted woman, Marie was also pathetically lonely. When the dashing Dr. Bertrand began paying a great deal of attention to her, he found little resistance.

Leo, however, still maintained his relationship with the much younger Ruth Bouchard while keeping company with the widow Charette; even Bertrand's marriage on September 3, 1951, to Marie Charette didn't damage his courtship of the prim Miss Bouchard.

Like most newlyweds, the Bertrands visited a lawyer to draw up new wills. Three days after their wedding, the couple bequeathed their estates to each other, as Ottawa barrister Aurele Parisien watched.

Later that fall, the energetic Bertrand took Ruth Bouchard and two of her ever-present sisters for a drive in the country. On the shores of Lac Ste. Marie, Quebec, he found an isolated cabin and made tentative arrangements to rent it for the week of November 10.

Bertrand drove to the cabin again on both November 8 and 9. But after his return from the third trip, he informed Ruth that he'd changed his mind about renting the cottage. However, he then proceeded to visit several friends, asking to borrow their camping supplies. He also picked up two five-gallon tins of Varsol.

A group of young men from the village of Lac Ste. Marie were heading to town as young men often will on a Saturday evening. There had been a heavy snowfall just days before, and even though it was only the second week in November, they soon realized they should not have started out without chains on their tires. As they approached a particularly hilly section of the back road, they decided to stop and put the chains on before attempting to proceed further.

As Dominic Newton secured the chains, he heard what he presumed were two gun shots. Shortly after, and now with increased traction, the group resumed their trip to town. Driving slowly because of the poor road conditions, they came upon a late-model, black Cadillac at the side of the road. The young men knew that at that point a trail led off in the direction of Mike Skahen's isolated cabin. They also knew he frequently rented it out to city slickers wanting a temporary retreat.

The Cadillac's engine idled, and a man stood beside it whose manner of dress caught their eyes. Dominic Newton and his friends rarely, if ever, saw a man dressed in an evening jacket, white shirt, and black bow tie, travelling the rural highways and byways. But they stopped to ask if he required assistance.

"You must help me," Bertrand implored, his face flushed and damp with perspiration. "My wife is in the Skahen cabin. A lamp exploded and she burned her hand. I came out to the car to get the spare sheets to make a dressing for her wound. When I got back to the cabin, it was on fire."

The young men assumed the injured woman lay in the back seat of the car, ready to be transported to the hospital. The group then offered to go to the cabin to see if anything could be salvaged from the disaster.

"It's too late," Bertrand advised. "It's completely gone. Just rubble, now."

At that point Bertrand returned to his Cadillac and got into the driver's seat. Assuming they couldn't be of any further help there, the young men resumed their drive to town. Bertrand's Cadillac followed close behind, which reassured the group of men. The road was a treacherous one, even for those familiar with it.

Not far along, a truck blocked the way. Dominic Newton recognized the truck as his father's. He told the man to hurry.

"There's a car right behind us. The man's wife's been badly burned. He's following us to the hospital in town."

Seconds later, Dr. Bertrand left his car to inquire about the delay.

"Don't worry, sir, this man's my father and I've told him to hurry because your wife needs medical attention," Dominic explained hurriedly.

"No, no, my wife's not in the car; she's still in the cabin. I'm simply going to the police station in Hull to advise them of the accident," Bertrand clarified coldly and returned to his car, leaving the others bewildered.

Leo Bertrand, never one to let the reactions of others dissuade him from his obligations, arrived at police clerk Joseph Deschenes's desk at 11:00 p.m.

After a full five minutes of meandering small talk, the doctor got to the point of his visit. Interestingly, Bertrand told Deschenes quite a different story than he'd told Dominic Newton and his chums. Later, Deschenes described Bertrand as having "not a bit of urgency about him."

"I had taken my wife camping to the Skahen cabin near Lake Ste. Marie.

We'd left the car at the side of the road and walked in, it would be about a quarter of a mile, I'd estimate. I left my wife in the cottage while I went back to get our luggage. Last I saw her she was lighting a Coleman lamp. It must have exploded because by the time I got back with our gear the place was in flames. She was still inside. It was burning so quickly there was really no way I could save her."

Joseph Deschenes phoned his superior. Detective John L. Ross headed up the Hull detachment of the Quebec Provincial Police (QPP) and lived only a few blocks from it. Ross, a seventeen-year police veteran, listened to Bertrand's almost verbatim re-telling of the incidents with appropriate objectivity.

As the pompous Bertrand now dealt with a police officer of some rank, not merely a clerk, he added, in a conspiratorial manner, that he trusted the investigation would be discreet. After all, he needed to consider his professional standing in the community.

By the time Bertrand left Detective Ross's office, it was a few minutes into Remembrance Day, Sunday, November 11. In spite of the lateness of the hour, Ross reported Bertrand's visit and the fire-related death of Mrs. Bertrand to his superiors in Montreal before returning home to bed. He'd have to be up early the next morning to meet the investigators sent from Montreal.

Bertrand returned home and spent Sunday visiting with various friends to whom he told much the same story of the incident. Later, there were only two variations of the story told. In one, he spoke of trying in vain to save his wife, and in the second version he held that he had seen the fire from the road and had known immediately the situation was hopeless.

Detective Ross welcomed Detective Sergeant Paul Coulcombe and Detective Merrill Lawton from the Montreal headquarters of the QPP early Sunday morning. After quickly briefing the two visitors about the reported fire, Ross summoned a squad car and the trio made their way to the Skahen property.

There the police noted several sets of prints in the snow: the tracks of a man and a woman leading away from the road and toward the burnt cabin in the woods, and a third set of prints made by the same male.

Beside those lone tracks, which indicated that the man was wearing overshoes, they found two circular indentations in the snow. About six metres further toward the cottage they found a wad of paper that smelled heavily of Varsol. Searching for further evidence the trio skirted the area surrounding what little remained of the cabin. The single set of tracks continued, stopping only at what would have been the front door of the little building. Ross noted no signs to indicate that anyone had stood watching the fire.

All that remained of the cabin was an outline of ashes, and five badly charred and still-warm wooden beams.

Detective Ross had visited the cabin a couple of years previously and he remembered that there had been a table against one wall and two wooden bunks against the opposite one. On what was left of one of the bunks, the officer now noted a grey outline in the ashes, an image shaped like a body and what they presumed had been the deceased's clothing. The head faced towards what had been the door of the one-room residence.

In an attempt to retrieve what little evidence remained, Ross bent to pick up the skull. It disintegrated at his touch as did every other major bone of what had been the newlywed Mrs. Bertrand's body. None of the three seasoned police officers had ever seen a body so completely consumed, but they collected what they could. When the police laboratory later weighed the poor woman's remains they amounted to a mere three pounds.

A Coleman lamp lay by the remains of the woman's feet, the lamp that Bertrand claimed exploded and started the tragic series of events. Strangely, it lay unbroken, completely undamaged, except blackened by the ravages of the fire. How could the lamp's glass be intact if the lamp exploded as Bertrand claimed?

Not far from the charred lamp they found two five-gallon cans lying on their sides. Like the lamp, the cans showed no signs of having exploded. Other evidence collected from the death scene included a hand pump used for lighting Coleman lamps, the head of an axe, a broken knife, and a few pieces of a broken bracelet.

The officers left the site knowing there was little doubt that the overly polite and extremely dapper Bertrand had murdered his wife in a disgustingly cold and calculated manner.

They contacted the suspect immediately. The ex-convict-cum-good-doctor was his usual charming self during the interview. During the forty-five-minute session, Bertrand spoke of many things. He took advantage of his captive audience and subjected Detective Ross to an opinionated critique of music.

He referred only once to his visit to the Hull police station the previous night. Bertrand explained that, understandably, the evening's events so traumatized him that he became somewhat confused in reporting the time which had elapsed while he stood watching the burning cabin. It was not a mere five minutes as he'd previously stated. Thirty minutes, he now felt would be a more accurate estimate.

"Flesh burns extremely quickly," he added with a pleasant smile.

Not surprisingly, police detained Leo Bertrand, and that afternoon sent both the suspect and the salvaged scraps of evidence to Montreal.

Further and extremely detailed investigations of what had been the Skahen cabin continued over the next two weeks, and a coroner's inquest was scheduled for November 26, 1951. Bertrand's mental and emotional states during this time are not recorded, but as he'd been granted freedom after his trial for the drowning death of his first wife, the gentleman's nature might have been unaffected. If so, his confidence was misplaced: Coroner Dr. Gerald Brisoon decreed that in his expert view the death of the second Mrs. Bertrand could not possibly have been accidental. In less than six minutes, the jurors at the inquest returned a verdict indicating their agreement, and Bertrand was charged with the murder of his fifty-three-year-old and wealthy wife, Marie Blanche Rosa Charette.

Mr. Justice Valmore Bienvenue called the criminal trial to order at 9:00 a.m. on Monday, February 11, 1952. Crown prosecutors were Noel Dorion and Availa Labelle. Lawyer for the defense was Jean Drapeau, who would go on to become one of the most outspoken and controversial mayors in Montreal's history. The defendant, Joseph Antoine Leo Real Bertrand, sat calmly in the prisoner's box for the third time in his thirty-nine years. He appeared somewhat detached from his surroundings and spent his time studiously taking notes of the events as they unfolded.

Monsieur Drapeau hotly contested many of the damning details presented by the prosecutors. A carefully selected cast of witnesses for the Crown countered. Many of these people related that the man they knew as Dr. Bertrand had been quite candid in revealing his plans to become financially secure by marrying a wealthy woman.

Such statements as "Within five years I should never have to work again" were credited to Leo Bertrand. His whirlwind romance with the late Marie Blanche Rosa Charette, while also courting the young school teacher Ruth Bouchard, was discussed at length, as were the wills witnessed by lawyer Aurele Parisien just days after Bertrand's marriage to Charette. The choice of the isolated Skahen cabin and the preparations Bertrand had made before the fatal camping trip also received considerable attention.

The accumulation of evidence against his client left defense attorney Jean Drapeau virtually powerless. As was his style, however, Drapeau frequently and flamboyantly argued with minor points, a tactic aimed at distracting the jury.

The assistant manager of the Lyle Blackwell dry-cleaning plant testified that his foreman, Leo Bertrand, had visited the plant twice on the day of the fire. On both occasions he'd been asking to borrow Varsol. Drapeau took this as an invitation to attack the importance of those requests.

"Did you actually see my client leaving with any Varsol?" Drapeau asked.

"No," the assistant manager admitted.

"And was any of your Varsol noted to be missing that afternoon?" the lawyer probed.

"No, well, I'm not sure actually. I didn't check really."

"So, you cannot state under oath that you know my client was in possession of any amount of Varsol, then can you?"

"No, sir, I'm afraid I cannot. I just know Leo Bertrand asked for Varsol twice last November 10," the dry-cleaning employee declared.

While Drapeau's tactics were dramatic, those of the Crown prosecutors' were thorough.

Detective Paul Coulcombe testified, in an unemotional recounting, to the sets of tracks that he and his colleagues had followed in the snow the day after the fire. The jury listened to his description of the sets of footprints leading to and from the cabin. The group of twelve was also clearly impressed when the salesman who had sold Bertrand his new overshoes appeared to testify.

Dominic Newton, the young man who'd come across Bertrand immediately following the fire, was anxious to be helpful — so anxious, in fact, that he tried to make the most emphatic impression he could during his time on the witness stand. He explained that while attaching chains to the tires of his vehicle he had heard two shots fired, seen a glow of fire, and smelled smoke. He also described speaking with the carefully attired Dr. Bertrand at the roadside.

Andrew Newton, Dominic's father, took the stand next. He testified that he had passed the Cadillac only moments before his son had and that he had seen neither smoke nor flames.

The younger Newton later withdrew the most colourful parts of his evidence.

The case had developed a large following in the press and the public. Popular opinion held Leo Bertrand guilty of killing his wife, if not wives. Despite the outsiders' preconceived notions, the trial progressed in the formal manner appropriate to the seriousness of the charge.

The medical-legal bureau of the QPP supplied four expert witnesses. Two chemists, Frenchere Pepin, with thirty years of experience, and Bertrand Peclet, whose reputation as a scientist had been established by his work on several criminal cases, testified that the Varsol that had soaked into the wad of paper which the police had found at the scene of the burned-out cabin exactly matched the formula used by the Lyle Blackwell dry-cleaning company. In addition, the size and shape of the wad matched the hole found in one of the cans at the scene of the tragic fire.

The scientists also explained with a clarity that must have been a knife wound in Bertrand's heart that the lamp could not have exploded and caused the fire. The lamp seized by the police not only had not exploded, but there were no traces of fuel in the lamp and, further, the valve that would have controlled the flow of fuel, had there been any, was shut tight when retrieved.

The last to add to the mounting pile of evidence were two medical practitioners. One of those, Dr. Jean Roussel, had twenty years experience, some of which had been gained during Leo Bertrand's 1935 trial for the murder of his first wife, the pregnant young Rose Anna Asseline Bertrand.

Dr. Rosario Fontaine, the other medical doctor involved in the investigation, had been the director of the Medical-Legal Bureau of the QPP. Unlike Dr. Bertrand's titles, both of these men's credentials were above reproach.

When she was alive, Mrs. Bertrand had weighed one hundred and fifty-five pounds. The fire had reduced her to a mere three pounds. The experts testified that the fire that had consumed her body had been fueled by more than just the materials that had gone into the construction of the cabin.

Even in intense fires of long duration, the larger portions of a body, such as the torso and buttocks, characteristically retain a good proportion of their size and bulk. They concluded that not only had the fire that consumed Mrs. Bertrand's body been promoted by the addition of a highly flammable material, this same material was doubtless applied directly and in large amounts to the victim's clothing. The two medical men agreed that Varsol was such a material.

Because so little of the body remained, neither practitioner was able to draw any conclusions about how the deceased met her end. She might have been shot, strangled, or beaten to death before the fire. No one would ever know.

On Monday, February 18, the Crown presented its final arguments to the jurors. Leo Bertrand's future did not look promising.

However, Jean Drapeau, foreshadowing his dramatic political career, captured the jurors' attentions. The Crown had not, he contented, proven that the woman who had once been the well-heeled widow Charette had been murdered. All that had been proven was that the second Mrs. Bertrand was dead and that her second husband, Leo Bertrand, had lied clumsily about his actions on the evening of her death.

By the time court heard the summations, it was late in the day, so Mr. Justice Valmore Bienvenue adjourned the court, setting the final session for nine o'clock the following morning. That decision, which seemed ordinary enough at the time, proved to be a fateful decree.

On Tuesday, as ordered, the colourful cast in this tragic drama reassembled and were listening carefully as the judge began his address to the jury. Not wanting to err in any matter concerning the complex case, Mr. Justice Bienvenue frequently referred to the lengthy notes he had prepared. Twenty-five minutes into the address, he made an initial reference to the weight of circumstantial evidence. He paused and picked up the glass of water set before him. As he lifted the glass to his lips, it slipped from his hand and shattered where it fell at his feet. Mr. Justice Bienvenue had suffered a fatal heart attack.

Mr. Justice Paul Ste. Marie, who was hearing a case in an adjoining courtroom, hurried in to adjourn court for the day advising jurors to report the next morning. By such time, he trusted that the attorney general would have some direction for those involved.

That decision was that the case would have to be re-tried. And so, as at his first trial for killing his first wife, Leo Bertrand's charges of wife-murderer would have to go to a second trial.

On Monday, May 12, 1952, the always-well-turned-out Leo Bertrand again sat in the prisoner's box, charged with the murder of his wife. Mr. Justice Francois Caron was on the bench. Noel Dorion and Availa Labelle returned as the prosecutors, but Jean Drapeau's flamboyant style would not contribute to Leo's defense this time. His lawyer was Joseph Ste. Marie.

Little new evidence was presented, but even that was distinctly damaging to Leo Bertrand's professed innocence. In case anyone should propose that the remains found in the fire-ravaged cabin were not that of Mrs. Bertrand, Detective Paul Coulcombe presented her false teeth, a locket, an earring, a dry-cell battery, and a ring with the initials ARC inscribed on it. The ring had been a memento that Marie Blanche Rosa Charette Bertrand had retained from her first marriage.

Nine days after this trial began, the jury retired to ponder the evidence. They spent less than half an hour deliberating before returning a verdict of "guilty as charged." The sentence was execution by hanging.

Incredibly, Leo Bertrand's face registered complete surprise. He clearly expected an acquittal. The pompous, natty, and self-aggrandizing man collapsed in shock. Guards supported Bertrand as they led him from the courtroom.

Friday, August 8, 1952, was determined as the day that the doctor would join his two wives in the hereafter. Bertrand's lawyer, however, launched a series of unsuccessful appeals that resulted in delaying the sentence.

During this time, Leo Bertrand worked feverishly to earn a release from the death sentence. He contacted Father D'Aoust, the priest he served during his term in the penitentiary at Prince Albert. He asked the elderly man to intercede on his behalf. Father D'Aoust declined.

Bertrand's next ploy was to feign insanity. This delayed the pathetic man's meeting with his maker by an additional two weeks. During those days, a court-appointed psychiatrist examined Bertrand and found that, except for entertaining delusions of his own importance, Leo Bertrand was completely sane.

As Thursday, June 11, 1953, became Friday, June 12, prison employees made final preparations at the gallows outside Montreal's famed Bordeaux Prison. They carefully checked the red metal scaffold which jutted out from a second-storey doorway overlooking the prison yard. Others led a decidedly unsteady Leo Bertrand from his cell on death row. Hangman Camille Branchaud adjusted the deadly contrivance on the convicted man's body. With practiced efficiency, Branchaud carried out the orders issued to him.

By 1:12 a.m., on the eve of his forty-first birthday, Joseph Antoine Leo Real Bertrand, alias the Tuxedo Kid and alias Dr. Bertrand, departed this world.

ALL IN THE FAMILY

"You've made a wise choice Raymond, my friend," car salesman Len Amoroso proclaimed as he handed the keys for a shiny, new, 1959, white Chevrolet Impala convertible to the young man standing beside him. "Once a fellow slips behind the wheel of an automobile like this, the world's at his feet."

The younger man said nothing. He merely stood smiling vacantly and staring at the car, possibly trying to convince himself that within minutes he really would be driving the flashy car off the lot and into his future.

Amoroso lowered his voice conspiratorially and continued, "You won't be riding around alone in this baby very often, if you catch my drift."

The salesman punctuated those closing thoughts with a friendly slap on his customer's shoulder. The touch appeared to waken the younger man from a daze.

"Oh, yeh, yeh, sure I know just what you mean."

"Well, then, away you go, Raymond. Enjoy your new car."

Amoroso waved as the new car-owner drove off the lot and onto Edmonton's 82 Avenue. Closing that deal not only meant a nice sales-commission cheque this month but the 1958 station wagon Cook had traded in should command a fair price too. Before any of that, though, he'd have to process the paperwork. What a time-consuming nuisance, one he'd just as soon ignore for now. Besides, tomorrow was Saturday and Saturdays were usually quiet, at least until noon.

Amoroso's young customer seemed a pleasant enough chap if a bit groggy. Why a few times when Len called him by his name, the youngster hadn't even responded right away. Perhaps the kid was tired; besides, what did any of that matter? The fellow held a steady job as a diesel mechanic in Red Deer, and even though the deal really didn't require strengthening, Len asked for and was given a deposit of $90 cash. Raymond Cook had quoted his salary as $750 a month. And while that amount provided a comfortable living, it would not have allowed him to throw nearly $100 away on a deal he didn't mean to complete.

The prescribed sales method had worked once again. All the information Amoroso needed he'd noted on the sales agreement. In keeping with his training, Amoroso had used Cook's driver's license as identification but kept it only long enough to jot down the data once. Complete the deal quickly, the sales manager preached. Let the customer's enthusiasm work for you. Collect the information you need expeditiously, wave a hearty good-bye to the new car owner, and then look after the details of the transaction.

But tomorrow morning would be plenty of time for that. So he spread the sheets out on his desk and closed his office door, knowing that everything he needed would be waiting for him sixteen hours later.

Amoroso's eagerness to earn the commission on one of the most expensive models available at Hood Motors may have effected the thoroughness with which he examined Cook's driver's license. If he'd given the document anything more than a cursory check, he'd have spotted a serious anomaly. The man who had just driven away in the convertible was a skinny, pimply faced kid. If he was out of his teens at all, it was only by a couple of years. The license belonged to someone born in 1908, making the owner of the document fifty-one years old.

Amoroso had surmised correctly that his customer was tired. The young man showed tell-tale signs of busy days and insufficient sleep. But that wasn't the only reason he had responded slowly to the name Raymond Cook. People usually called him Bob or Bobby, his full name being Robert Raymond Cook. The driver's license belonged to his patient and beleaguered father.

When Amoroso arrived at work the next morning, he paused only long enough to pour himself a cup of coffee before going to his office to leaf through the documents from his profitable sale. He then noticed Cook's signature missing from the insurance contract. This meant that somewhere out there a young man was driving around without car insurance.

The salesman certainly didn't want to drive all the way to Cook's home to get the papers signed. Even if he hurried, Amoroso knew the trip would use up most of his day. Stettler, sixty miles east of Red Deer, was over a hundred miles from Edmonton, and spending the last Saturday in June travelling the back roads of central Alberta didn't hold much appeal. After a moment's thought, he phoned the RCMP in Cook's home town and explained the situation to them.

As a courtesy, Sergeant Tom Roach agreed to have his men keep an eye out for the car. They'd have no trouble spotting it on the streets of this quiet community. Besides, most of the policemen in the area knew the Cook family, especially the eldest son, Robert.

Most of the townspeople agreed with the police force's opinion about the youngster: nothing but a nuisance that kid, and getting worse; into trouble pretty regular now for years; the first time the boy slept behind bars he wasn't even sixteen; since then he'd rarely stayed out of jail for more than a month at a time. As a result no one, except Robert's father, had really missed Bob these past three years, while the apparently incorrigible youth served a well-deserved sentence for robbery in the Prince Albert Penitentiary in Saskatchewan.

As Constable Allan Eugene Braden wheeled his police cruiser onto Stettler's Main Street, he noted the convertible his boss had asked him to locate. He drove alongside the shiny new car and couldn't help but admire it. As he approached the driver, he second guessed the wisdom of his career decisions. On his wages he could never afford such a luxurious automobile.

"Are you Raymond Cook?" he asked.

The young man with slicked back, light brown hair answered with a nod.

"The sergeant needs to see you."

Again Cook nodded in agreement. The two cars made U-turns and headed to the detachment offices where Cook appeared calm and confident, like a man with nothing to hide.

Sergeant Roach looked forward to Ray Cook, Bob's father, coming into the office. That's the name the car salesman from Edmonton had given him. Roach knew the man and wondered why a sensible, hard-working family man who talked of nothing but saving money toward buying his own garage would blow his money on such an extravagant car. It didn't fit with the Ray Cook that Roach knew. And as he watched Bobby Cook walk into the station, just ahead of Constable Braden, the veteran police officer's discomfort increased. Previous experience with those feelings told him he'd soon be dealing with much more than an uninsured car.

Roach opened the gate beside the counter, inviting Cook in. He dismissed the constable with a curt, "Thanks, Al, I'll look after Mr. Cook now."

"Bob, I wasn't expecting you back home so soon. Is your term finished?" the cop inquired.

"They let a bunch of us go early, on accounta the Seaway opening down east and the Queen coming and stuff."

Tom Roach stared blankly at the man now sitting beside his desk. He knew that some fool, with no knowledge of policing, had extended an amnesty of one month per year of sentence to convicts in Her Majesty's prisons. Roach couldn't imagine what the connection was between a criminal and either the opening of the St. Lawrence Seaway or Queen Elizabeth and Prince Charles's visit to Canada. Unfortunately, no one had asked Roach for his opinion and more than 100 convicts serving their last months of prison terms happily accepted early releases.

Because Bob Cook's name rarely crossed the sergeant's mind once they'd gotten the trouble-maker behind bars, it hadn't occurred to Roach that a foolish ruling, made in Ottawa, might create a problem in his isolated prairie jurisdiction. The realization came so suddenly that it took him a moment to re-orient his thinking.

"Bob, where's your father? Why did you use his driver's license when you bought that car?" Roach probed.

"Dad and Daisy and the kids have gone on to B.C. Dad finally got that garage like he's been wanting," Robert Cook explained. "They've gone on ahead and I'll join them in a couple of days."

Cook's apparently relaxed words sparked a warning in the policeman's mind. Conning a commissioned salesman hadn't presented much of a problem for the smooth-talking youth, but Roach's mind worked quite differently. His suspicions increased as he listened to this known ne'er-do-well.

"Where did your father purchase the garage, Bob?"

"I told you, in B.C."

"But where in B.C. and how are they getting there?" The Mountie began to show signs of annoyance.

"They took the train," Cook answered obliquely.

The sergeant's patience strained visibly by now. This ex-convict's attempts to be elusive were more than this policeman intended to put up with.

"Where, Bob? Where did your parents go? What's the name of the town or city where your father bought the garage? If I wanted to write to him how would I address the letter? Where in B.C. did they go?"

"Oh, sorry, Sergeant Roach. I see what you mean now. They didn't actually tell me exactly where they were heading. Just that Dad bought a garage in B.C. and they'd call for me once they were settled," Robert replied calmly.

Roach knew that despite years of increasingly serious trouble the boy had been in, Ray had maintained a lenient and optimistic attitude toward his eldest son.

Young Bobby's mother had died in her twenties and her death had devastated Ray. He mourned deeply for his beloved Josephine. Little Bobby was the only connection left with her. Sadly, that link implied a tremendous responsibility — the onus of raising their son. Raymond Cook felt, with some justification, unequal to the task. Bob proved to be a difficult child who caused a great deal of trouble for his father and anyone else who tried to deal with him.

And so Ray hadn't been surprised when Bob's classroom teacher asked to see him. Even Daisy Gaspar, an experienced teacher and an effective disciplinarian, felt at a loss to curb the lad's disruptive behaviour. Oddly, not long after that meeting, Miss Gaspar became the second Mrs. Raymond Cook, thereby assuming far greater responsibility for the headstrong, badly behaved boy.

"Okay, we'll get back to that," Roach said. "Tell me why you had your father's driver's license. It seems to me he'll need it when he gets to this unknown destination."

"I'll send it to him right away, then," Bob answered. "He gave it to me because he thought I'd have an easier time buying the car with his identification."

"Your father knew you were going to buy this car then, did he?"

"Yeah, sure, Sergeant Roach. He even gave me his station wagon as a trade 'cause, see, I gave him quite a bit of cash. I'd sorta tucked away a bit from my last job."

"Bob, are you telling me your father accepted money you'd stolen to buy the business he'd been saving for?" Roach's voice rose.

The ridiculousness of the scenario presented by this young man increased by the minute.

"Look, Sergeant, me and my Dad both felt I'd paid for that money. He didn't feel bad taking it. I'd served my time for stealing it, now it was mine to give. In exchange he gave me the family car."

Roach didn't accept any of this. What he needed now was a reason to detain Cook.

"Bob, none of what you're saying makes any sense and I think you're well aware of that. I'm sorry but I'm going to have to arrest you."

"What for?" Cook yelled, jumping up from his chair. "I didn't do nothin'."

"You're charged with fraud. You purchased that car under false pretenses," Sergeant Roach explained as he led the angry young man to the cells below.

This arrest even broke Robert Cook's own record — back in jail, this time only four days after his release.

The shiny new Impala that Len Amoroso had predicted would bring Cook nothing but good times now sat locked in the garage under the Stettler post office, waiting to be searched. Sergeant Roach then called in two of his officers and informed them they'd be accompanying him on a trip to Raymond Cook's home at 5018 52 Street.

They knocked on the front door of the neatly kept, green-and-white bungalow. No one answered. Roach turned the knob and pushed the door open. The three officers entered, calling out to the family or whomever might be in the house. It was nearly 11 p.m. by now, and even though the summer solstice was only a few days past, the officers needed the flashlights they'd brought to help them around the unknown house.

This first cursory inspection looked as though Robert Cook's account actually occurred. The living room and kitchen were neat. There appeared to be little out of place. The family seemed merely to be away.

Sergeant Tom Roach, however, couldn't shake his conviction that something wasn't right. The officers closed up the house and returned to the detachment. Roach sent the two constables home for the night after asking them to be back at the station by nine the next morning. But before Roach left, he called his commanding officer, Staff Sergeant Dave Beeching, in Red Deer.

By nine Sunday morning, a team of RCMP specialists gathered around Roach's desk waiting for instructions. Beeching brought Constable George Sproule and Corporals Joseph Van Blarcom and Denis Novikoff with him to the hastily-called meeting. During the drive from Red Deer, he had briefed them as thoroughly as he was able, and now the three set out with a Stettler constable named Morrison to visit the Cook home, while Roach and Beeching remained at the detachment office.

From the exterior the bungalow looked recently tended but vacant. When no one answered their knocks, the officers entered the home through the unlocked front door. Clearly no one was home. The Saturday, June 27, edition of the *Calgary Herald* lay just inside the front porch door, indicating that no one had been at home the previous day either. Perhaps Robert Cook told the truth; perhaps the family had left early Friday morning for their new home in British Columbia. On initial inspection nothing at all appeared to be out of the ordinary at 5018 52 Street in Stettler.

Police eyes, however, rarely relax after an initial inspection, and before the officers left the living room, Constable Sproule began taking photographs. He knew these would never find a place in *House Beautiful*, but the decor wasn't what he focused on. It was the spots of dark discolouration on the television, the floor, the lampshade, even the wall just inches from the ceiling that he captured on film.

The group then moved into an adjoining bedroom which reflected none of the orderliness of the living room. A double bed, a chest of drawers, and a set of bunk beds stood in disarray. There were no sheets on any of the beds. Clothes were strewn onto the double bed, and bureau drawers stood open, revealing complete disorder. Two pairs of children's running shoes lay beside the bunk beds. A third pair of shoes, men's oxfords, were between the double bed and the bureau. Sproule began snapping pictures again. The mess in the room concerned him because it was in such contradiction to the neatness of the living room. Then a large dark stain on the toe of the man's shoe made his heart sink. It closely resembled the stains they'd noted in the living room.

As Corporal Novikoff lifted the clothing strewn about on the double bed, he let out an involuntary gasp. His teammates waited a moment and when the identification specialist remained silent, Van Blarcom asked:

"What? What have you got there, Denis?"

Almost before he finished the question, Joe Van Blarcom and the others could see for themselves. A shotgun lay buried among the clothes, which also hid two large, circular blood stains.

"It's still damp," Novikoff announced quietly as he pressed his hand against one of the stains. "We'd better let Roach and Beeching know right away."

In unspoken agreement, Constable Morrison left the blood-stained house and drove the cruiser back to the detachment offices.

Novikoff silently picked tiny chips from the soiled mattress.

"You'd better leave those," Van Blarcom advised. He knew the commanding officers would want to see the bone fragments exactly as they lay. "Let's get to the rest of the house."

The closet in this bedroom led to the second bedroom, which also contained two beds — a double and a single. There were stains on the bedroom walls, but someone had attempted to remove the largest ones. The unknown cleaner had only succeeded in smudging the area. The single bed had two mattresses stacked on it. Van Blarcom flipped the top one up on its side. In doing so, he found what he'd hoped he wouldn't — another large, circular blood stain. He later reported, in a classic cop-understatement style, "We then had good reason to believe there was something wrong."

A detailed investigation of the house began as soon as the senior officers arrived. Sproule painstakingly dusted the shotgun for fingerprints. There were none but the examination still proved worthwhile. Not only was the gun more of a collector's item than a weapon, but the barrel was bent in two places, most of the wooden stock was missing, and the hammer mechanism was broken. While all this evidence rated, and received, notation, the bits of hair and flesh which adhered to the gun's hammer created considerably more excitement among the veteran police officers.

Setting aside the gun and the piles of clothes, the men lifted the blood-soaked mattress. Under it lay a red necktie, a torn white shirt, and a man's pale blue suit. The lapels and sleeves of the jacket bore the now-familiar bloodstains, as did the trouser legs, zipper, and crotch areas. Five shotgun shells lay in the pockets. The shirt was new enough that the size markings were still easy to read — fifteen-inch neck, thirty-one-inch sleeve. A laundry mark spelling out the name ROSS also showed, although it was evident this shirt hadn't been anywhere near a laundry recently nor would it ever go there again. It was badly ripped and filthy.

Feeling relieved to be away from the traumatic sights in the bedrooms, the police continued their search, this time in the kitchen. A beer bottle clear of fingerprints stood on the counter. Otherwise the orderliness of the kitchen stood in mute and eerie contradiction to the evidence of violence in the bedrooms. Fearing the worst, the investigators proceeded down the basement stairs. They didn't know what to expect but, even so, what they found surprised them — an orderly, although slightly dusty, apartment. They climbed back up the stairs still wondering where the Cooks could be and what had happened in their house.

The only other building on the property was a garage. In order to let in as much light as possible, the men opened the large sliding door. Tires, car parts, garbage cans, a workbench and single-shot rifles lay scattered about.

When Sproule lifted the lid off one of the garbage cans, he found a towel, a mat and a blanket, all bloodstained, crammed into the container.

The cement floor had been covered with pieces of cardboard, evidently to protect it from oil stains. One piece at a time, the officers lifted up the cardboard, under which they found only clean cement until they came to the middle of the floor. Removing the protective cardboard here revealed wooden planks. It also allowed a nauseating smell to begin filtering out from between the planks. Even with the fresh air coming in from the open door, the officers instantly recognized the sickening odour of decaying flesh. Silently, the two constables lifted up the planks to view the grease pit below.

"George," the staff sergeant from Red Deer called to the photographer, "You'd better get in here before we go any further. We'll need pictures of each step here. And someone better head on back to the station. Cook should be well guarded. I think we've just found his parents."

No one spoke for a time, while the realization of what happened registered.

"We'd better get the funeral home over here. They'll know the best way to remove the bodies," Roach commented.

"Bodies?" asked Van Blarcom. "There's more than one?"

"Yup, they're both here," Roach confirmed, and he turned from the stench in the pit and walked out of the garage. Kicking pointlessly at the dry ground beneath his feet, the sergeant continued, "I wonder where the kids are though. Maybe they sent them ahead to wherever they planned on settling in B.C. I think Ray's sister lives in Hanna. She'll know. Poor woman will probably be the one who'll have to tell those children. They had five, didn't they, five other kids? "

"They're orphans now, I guess," the corporal said staring at the ground. "The two little girls aren't much more than babies, if I remember right. Hard to believe such a thing'd happen here."

A young man walked up the driveway toward the policemen.

"Good morning, sir," the youth offered tentatively. "I'm Dillon Hoskins, a friend of Bobby Cook's. Is anything wrong?"

"Hello, Dillon," Van Blarcom replied. "Yes, I'm afraid quite a bit's wrong, but first of all what brings you here just now?"

"My father does, sir. See, we got this call from Bob. He said you've got him in lock-up because he used his father's I.D. to buy a car. He wants us to post bail, but Dad kinda wondered how Mr. Cook would feel if he did. See Ray Cook, he's usually pretty good to Bob, and Dad figured if Ray wasn't posting bail himself then maybe there was a reason," Hoskins explained haltingly.

Although he had nothing to hide from the police, Dillon felt distinctly uncomfortable in their presence. He'd already identified himself as a friend of Bob Cook's. They might suspect he was involved somehow with buying the car.

"Your father's right," Sergeant Roach interjected. "There's a very good reason why Ray Cook hasn't posted bail for Bob, but we can't get into that just yet. Have you seen Bob recently?"

"Yeah, Thursday, I think it was. I seen him walking along the highway toward town. He musta caught a lift with somebody cause a truck was just pulling away and he was waving to the driver."

"Would you mind coming into the house with me?" Roach asked. "Perhaps you could identify a couple of things for me."

Confused and concerned, Dillon Hoskins wondered if maybe his parents weren't right. Maybe Bobby Cook really was nothing but trouble. Although they had never been what you could call close friends, Hoskins had always secretly admired Cook's nerve and his ability to get away with things that other guys in town would have been afraid even to try.

Coming in out of the bright sunlight, it took young Dillon Hoskins's eyes a few minutes to adjust. By that time, he and Sergeant Roach stood in one of the bedrooms in the Cook house.

"Dillon, have you ever seen this suit before?" the cop asked.

"Oh, my god, what happened to it?" Hoskins stammered.

"You mean the blood?" Roach asked rhetorically. "We're not sure yet. But have you ever seen it before? Can you answer my question?"

Dillon Hoskins only stared uncomprehendingly at the clothes.

"Have you ever seen this suit before?" the sergeant repeated with barely concealed impatience.

"Yes. Yes, I think I have. It looks like the one Bobby was wearing when I saw him Thursday. He had on a suit and a white shirt and a red tie. I remember thinking he looked pretty good."

Voices from the outside interrupted the conversation.

"I think you'd better be on your way now, Dillon. Stay in touch though. If you're going to leave town be sure and let us know first, will you?"

"Yeah, sure," the young man replied as the two walked back outside.

"Thank your father for his concern. If we need him, we'll be sure to call," the officer promised.

Dillon Hoskins made his way down the Cooks' driveway and past the hearse from Brennan's Funeral Home. He gave a final glance back at the house, the police cruiser, the hearse, and the half dozen troubled-looking men standing between the house and the garage. An involuntary shiver that ran through his body prompted him to break into a run.

"I guess Van Blarcom explained why we need you," Roach addressed the men who'd arrived in the hearse. "I'll show you what we've found."

Despite the amount of decomposition, the police and funeral-home workers all agreed the first body retrieved was that of Raymond Cook. The second body, they assumed, belonged to Daisy Cook, although for the moment it was impossible to be sure — little of the woman's face remained.

The stench and sight of the bodies were nearly unbearable, so they worked quickly. Only by getting the remains into refrigerated morgue compartments could they expect any relief.

"On three," Roach directed as the two undertakers squatted beside the grease pit in preparation to remove the second body. "One. Two. Three."

Roach had barely uttered the last syllable when raw horror took his voice away. There, hidden beneath the two adult-size bodies, lay smaller bodies, lots of them. The five children the officers had discussed earlier had not gone ahead to their new home. They had not gone anywhere, for here, clad only in pajamas, were their small corpses.

Fighting waves of nausea, the police helped the funeral-home workers remove the pathetic remains. Hurrying wouldn't save any lives at this point but, still, an increased sense of urgency set in. People needed to be contacted, reports made. Bob Cook's lawyer would have to be called, as would the coroner's office. Best to get as much as possible accomplished before the inevitable reporters arrived.

"Just hold these," Roach instructed the undertakers, indicating the bodies. "I have no idea who the coroner-on-call is this weekend, but I'm sure he'll be here by tomorrow."

Knowing a great deal of police work awaited him, Roach headed back to the detachment offices, leaving Corporal Van Blarcom to cordon off the area.

Bob Cook knew something was afoot. From his cell directly under the sergeant's office, he heard pieces of conversation, and he realized from the amount of traffic in and out of the station that something out of the ordinary was going on.

When Roach charged him with false pretenses, Cook had contacted David MacNaughton, a lawyer in Edmonton. Much to Cook's surprise, and adding to the afternoon's commotion, MacNaughton arrived at his cell door. Surely such a charge didn't warrant a Sunday afternoon trip to Stettler.

Standing beside the attorney, Roach informed Robert Cook that they'd found the bodies of his father, stepmother and five half brothers and sisters.

Roach had barely spoken the formal charge when the prisoner became hysterical.

"Not my father, no, not my father," Cook uttered over and over again.

Finally, Roach and MacNaughton left the inconsolable young man to come to terms with what, to him, was apparently news. When they returned to Cook's cell about an hour later, he'd regained his composure and listened to the charges against him without comment. Leaving the guard posted by the cell area, Roach and MacNaughton left the police station to meet Dr. Peter Davey, a pathologist from the Royal Alexandra Hospital in Edmonton. The findings of his post-mortem examination would be very important to both the lawyer and the police officer, and they wanted to meet this man.

Stettler RCMP officer walks past the grease pit in the Cook family's garage, where, just hours before, police had made their grisly find.

(Courtesy of the Glenbow Archives, Calgary.)

Davey knew when he left Edmonton that he'd be working well into the night. A thorough examination of seven bodies is a time consuming process. He'd begun as soon as he'd reached the Brennan Funeral Home.

"I'm sure they all died at the same time," he confirmed moments after he began his examination. "Somewhere between twenty-four and ninety-six hours prior to this examination."

As the coroner's investigation continued, information concerning the time and cause of death came sporadically. Both deceased adults had died as a result of shotgun wounds, Raymond to his chest and Daisy to her head. The youngsters had all been beaten to death. Further proof had fallen from the sheet that the older of the girls was wrapped in. Two wood fragments, which matched the damaged handle of the shotgun police had found at the murder scene, lay beside four-and-a-half-year-old Kathy Cook's body.

By the next morning, the doctor's repulsive task was completed, and arrangements were made for Raymond Cook's cousins, Ralph and Charles Cudmore, to identify the bodies. As they carried out their unenviable task, a listless and withdrawn Robert Cook stood, heavily guarded, in the Stettler courthouse. Magistrate H. F. Biggs read the charges against young Cook, who displayed no emotion. This was in stark contrast to his wildly emotional reaction when told of his family's death. Also, during his recent days in the pen, Cook had been involved in a fight which had earned him a head wound. All this caused the magistrate to order a thirty-day remand. Biggs wanted a full psychiatric assessment done before proceeding.

In addition to the obvious wisdom of the judge's decision in terms of the legal process, sending the prisoner to nearby Ponoka's mental hospital meant one less task for the local police. The responsibility for guarding Robert Cook now rested with the hospital's forensic unit and freed Sergeant Roach to assemble evidence for the Crown's case.

Word of the event brought reporters and photographers from all over the country flocking to Stettler, a town they'd likely never heard of twenty-four hours earlier. Even the usually business-like *Globe and Mail* carried the following dramatic headline on Monday, June 29, 1959 — "Find Alberta Family of 7 Slain in Garage Near Home."

While a constable drove the handcuffed Cook north to the hospital, as ordered by the magistrate, Corporals Van Blarcom and Novikoff headed east to the RCMP crime laboratory in Regina. They carried blood-soaked evidence for examination by serologists, specialists in such investigations. All three police officers knew they needed to get back to Stettler quickly. Now, in addition to their routine work, they needed to collect evidence so the Crown's case would be ready by the trial date, July 29, 1959.

The bulk of this investigation centered around Bob Cook's movements from the time of his release (from the Prince Albert Penitentiary) on Tuesday, June 23, until the following Saturday when Constable Braden escorted him into the police station. Cook freely admitted that he'd spent his first day of freedom drinking with his former, fellow inmate, Jim Myhaluk. The two had travelled together from the penitentiary to Saskatoon where they proceeded to tour beer parlors.

On the Wednesday, just after 6 a.m., slightly the worse for wear, the pair arrived in Edmonton, set on continuing their exploration of drinking establishments. Finding they were a tad early for such activity, they took a cab to the city's south side. Myhaluk went to his parents' home, and Cook rented a room at the Commercial Hotel. When questioned by police, Myhaluk stated that he hadn't seen Cook again until evening, when Bob dropped in for a moment before continuing downtown in search of friends. The amnesty ruling, which released so many prisoners on the same day, meant that cities and towns within a day's travel from Prince Albert were veritable hotbeds of activity for small-time hoods, many of whom Cook knew from one or another of his frequent stays behind bars. Before long, something of an old-boys reunion developed. Cook and another former inmate, Walter Berezowski, partied the night away in several seedy Edmonton hotels.

Berezowski cooperated fully with the police when they found him. He explained that Cook was anxious to get home to Stettler the next day, Thursday, as his father had promised to give him a car in celebration of completing his jail term. To help his friend, Berezowski borrowed a truck and drove Cook from Edmonton to Stettler. The two had spent a few hours driving around Cook's home town before they parted company. Berezowski headed back to Edmonton to return the vehicle, after leaving Bob Cook at the side of the highway on the edge of town. This is where Dillon Hoskins reported first seeing Cook. Hoskins recalled that Cook wore a pale blue suit, white shirt, and red tie. He also remembered Cook being empty handed at the time.

Other law-abiding citizens of Stettler told police they'd seen Robert Cook around town on and off until Thursday evening. One man explained that sometime between 8:30 and 9:15, he had been watching when Ray Cook apparently first noticed his son's arrival in town. The witness remembered the elder Cook swinging his car into the curb and hurrying to his son's side. By observing the two, the man deduced that Ray was much more enthusiastic about the meeting than his son was.

Dillon Hoskins' parents, Leona and Jim, described visiting in the Cook home until approximately nine o'clock on Thursday evening. All seemed in order when they left. Although the little bungalow was for sale, neither Ray nor Daisy gave any indication that a sale was either imminent or urgent. If the

Cooks intended to leave for B.C. the next day, they didn't mention the plan to the Hoskins. Rather, Ray Cook had volunteered to help the Hoskins move furniture on Saturday afternoon, and plans were finalized for the two families to picnic together on Sunday.

Re-creating the chain of events up to approximately nine o'clock Thursday evening hadn't proved much of a challenge; however, at that point, the trail ran out. Further inquiry only confirmed that while Ray Cook spoke occasionally of buying a vehicle repair shop and Daisy liked the idea of moving to British Columbia, neither expressed any particular sense of urgency about the change. Quite the contrary: in addition to helping his friend Hoskins move furniture and joining the family outing Sunday, Ray Cook had arranged to work on a specific car on Saturday morning. People knew him to be a man who kept his word.

Stettler's milkman, a man named Larson, explained that Daisy Cook purchased five dollars' worth of milk tickets Thursday. Even with a large family she couldn't have expected to use that much milk in just a day. With each new report, Robert's story of his family's decision to move to British Columbia became increasingly suspect. Because no one saw any member of the Cook household, except Robert, alive after 9 p.m. Thursday, June 25, the police needed to find out where the young man spent the night.

A co-worker of Ray Cook's testified that he drove past the bungalow at 8:15 Friday morning, and he had noted Cook's station wagon wasn't in the driveway. That didn't seem odd to the man until he arrived at work. Cook wasn't there, nor had he phoned to explain his absence. At almost exactly that time, roughly a hundred miles north, Bob Cook, armed with his father's identification, visited car dealerships in search of a more impressive car than the family wagon. By 9:30 that morning, Jim Myhaluk joined Bob. By noon they were finalizing the purchase of a white, 1959 Chev Impala convertible from Len Amoroso, salesman at Hood Motors.

"The car won't be ready for you to pick up till later this afternoon," Amoroso informed the man he knew as Ray Cook. "Why don't you boys find a place to catch a couple hours sleep. You both look pretty tired."

According to Myhaluk, the two disregarded the man's suggestion and instead "bummed around town" with a third friend, while waiting for the car. Cook went back to the dealership by himself and, shortly after, cruised past the nearby Commercial Hotel to show off his new car. He advised Jim that he was heading back to Stettler, anxious to impress the people in town with his extravagant purchase. Myhaluk explained that he didn't give Cook or his whereabouts another thought until Sunday when he learned from a radio broadcast of the young man's arrest.

A news bulletin of the gruesome find in the Cook's garage brought a call to Stettler's finest from Camrose, a neighbouring town. Constable John Bell recognized the name Raymond Cook. The constable had dealt with "Raymond Cook" and his flashy convertible no fewer than three times from 8 p.m. Friday evening until just after four Saturday afternoon. The last time Bell saw Cook he charged him with supplying liquor to minors and invited him to leave town immediately.

The charge related to a small group of teenagers Cook befriended while visiting Camrose. The youngsters explained they'd been with Cook from about 7:30 on Friday evening until four o'clock the following afternoon. During that time all were drinking heavily and joy riding around the province in Cook's new car. Just a few hours later, Constable Braden spotted Cook driving around Stettler and brought the young man in as Sergeant Roach had asked.

When the Stettler police held Cook in their cells, first on a false pretense charge and then awaiting his arraignment on the murder charge, it marked the incorrigible youth's seventh jail sentence. He had served time in jails all across the Canadian prairies, mostly on theft-related charges, but he had shown no history of violence in his dealings, except the fight in jail, which had resulted in nearly thirty stitches to repair a gash on his head. Oddly, prison life seemed to suit Cook in a way that life on the streets never did. His fellow inmates liked him and enjoyed his many stories, especially the ones about the cache of money buried in Bowden, Alberta, where he'd done his last "job."

Despite all the time he spent in jail, Robert Cook had never tried to break out. However, the Ponoka mental hospital apparently didn't give Cook an equivalent sense of home: just before midnight on Thursday, July 10, Cook escaped from his hospital cell. A panicked guard reported he'd seen Cook lying on his cot reading at the 11:30 p.m. inspection, and so the escapee had no more than a half an hour's head start on the authorities. The RCMP called out every available officer and set up road blocks on all the arteries leading from the hospital. Within two hours their tactics were rewarded. The officers blocking Highway 12 to Stettler saw a fast-moving car bearing down on them. The car slowed as though in anticipation of stopping. One of the constables left the cruiser in preparation for stopping this vehicle and identifying its driver — a move that nearly cost the policeman his life. The approaching car suddenly sped up and careened around the blockade. The police gave chase in their cruisers and were gaining on the fleeing car when it missed a curve in the road, hit a fence and a dirt embankment, flew through the air an estimated sixty feet, and landed on its roof in a farmer's field.

Slamming on the brakes, one officer remarked to the other, "I guess this ends the Cook case."

The two made their way quickly to the wreck. Its wheels were still spinning as the officers crouched down, ready to pull Robert Cook's body free from the tangle of metal.

"My god, he's not there," the first man exclaimed as he peered into the dark and nearly flattened interior.

The second officer shone his flashlight around what had been the cab of the car, confirming his partner's incredible but accurate assessment. A quick search of the glove compartment turned up the car's ownership papers, and at 2:30 Saturday morning they woke the car's owner to inform him that his vehicle lay ruined in a field not far from his home in Ponoka.

By dawn, police established a mobile search headquarters near the scene of the accident. From here they guided the movements of the more than one hundred searchers called in to help find and apprehend Robert Cook. Road blocks continued in place, and four small planes circled the area although patches of dense bush severely limited visibility from the air.

Reporters from all over Canada repeated their pilgrimage to the Stettler area. They couldn't miss anything as dramatic as this manhunt to recapture the young man suspected of murdering his family. From Calgary to Edmonton, the citizens of Alberta prepared to protect themselves from Robert Cook. Even today, more than thirty years later, those who lived through the drama recall their reactions.

"I remember no one was allowed out to play," said one man.

"My parents were really frightened," another offered. "I wasn't born then but they say they wouldn't let my sisters out of the house until it was over."

The tension was highest in the town of Stettler. Robert Cook's escape proved his guilt in many people's minds. They loaded their rifles or asked for additional police protection. A special guard stood watch over the homes of Magistrate Biggs, who'd ordered Cook sent to the hospital, and Jim Hoskins, who had expressed concern that, because he'd turned down Bob's original request for bail money, the escapee might seek revenge.

RCMP Superintendent J.S. Cruickshank, of Edmonton's K division headquarters, sent an inspector to assist Staff Sergeant David Beeching in organizing the manhunt.

Sloughs littered the countryside and searchers waded through each one, but they found no trace of Cook. Tempers flared and efficiency suffered as lack of sleep and ninety-degree heat took its toll. Cruickshank called on a nearby military forces base to supply fresh personnel. The Provost Corps responded quickly, relieving the first frustrated group.

Every hour of his freedom cost Cook dearly in terms of any sympathy he might have had from the people in Stettler and the surrounding communities. The longer he remained on the lam, the more guilt town gossippers piled on him. Typical of such group mentality and skewed thinking, Cook's flight confirmed their worst suspicions.

A searcher found a slipper in a field near the town of Alix, thirty miles south east of Ponoka. He turned it over to his commanding officer, and a check with the hospital confirmed that it closely resembled the type issued to Cook at his admission. The hunt narrowed, focusing on the nearby area surrounding the spot where they'd found the slipper. Despite the intensity of the search, Robert Cook continued to elude capture.

At 7:30 p.m., July 12, the caretaker of a community hall not far from Alix unlocked the building in preparation for the weekly Saturday night dance. The hall bore distinct markings of a break-in: a window stood open and food was missing. The caretaker called the police.

The break-in indicated that Cook was travelling in a northwest path away from Stettler, possibly toward his friends in Edmonton. The police brought in tracking dogs, and within two miles of the vandalized community hall their strategy was partly rewarded. One of the dogs led its handler to a swatch of white-striped flannelette cloth caught on a fence surrounding a farmer's field. The material matched the pajamas Cook wore when the guard confirmed his presence at the 11:30 p.m. bed check.

When twilight gave way to nightfall, the commanding officers called their men in. This assured Cook's freedom until daybreak. But Cook clearly wanted more than to remain hidden; he wanted to escape. Toward that end, he visited Jennings Garage in Alix, leaving with a 1957 Monarch and a full tank of fuel for the car from Jennings's unlocked gas pumps. Troops who complemented the police established roadblocks at every conceivable route, but the fugitive remained at large.

Like everyone in the province, and for that matter most of the country, Richard Schultz, who farmed in the area surrounding Ponoka, kept his radio on to hear up-to-the-minute progress reports. When his wife spotted an abandoned car matching the description of the one reported stolen the night before, Schultz called the police. As soon as they confirmed the sighting, they knew Cook was back on foot. Again, nightfall postponed the manhunt, but the police re-located their search headquarters to the Schultz farm.

Early Tuesday morning, when local farmer Oscar Utas headed out to start his day's work, he noticed a granary door showed signs of being forced open. While hurrying back to the house, he glimpsed a shadowy figure around the side of a barn. Wisely, Utas ushered his family into the car and fled. He called police from the first pay phone he saw, but by the time authorities reached the property, Cook was gone.

Later, when neighbouring farmer Norman Dufva, going about his chores, spotted a man behind his pig barn, he also didn't investigate further; he called the police. The inspector heading the hunt, accompanied by three constables, arrived on the scene within minutes.

Standing in the yard between Dufva's house and barn, Inspector Laberge called out to Cook. He waited a minute and then called Cook a second time, assuring the fugitive that if he showed himself unarmed and peacefully he wouldn't be harmed. Seconds later, a shirtless Robert Cook made his way slowly toward the officers. Moments later he collapsed from exhaustion. After nearly eighty-eight hours on the run and successfully evading hundreds of searchers, Robert Cook was back in custody.

Word spread quickly throughout the communities. As the military retreated to their base at Wainwright, a hundred and fifty miles northeast, crowds of curious and relieved locals gathered to catch a glimpse of the man responsible for terrorizing the usually staid area. To their surprise, the worn-out youth they saw getting into the police cruiser looked considerably more pathetic than frightening.

Inspector Laberge and two other officers headed back to Edmonton with the prisoner handcuffed and sleeping in the back of the police car. They held him there in cells overnight, but first thing in the morning, they drove Cook to the federal penitentiary in Fort Saskatchewan, north-east of Edmonton.

Cook's escape meant that his preliminary hearing, originally scheduled for July 29, 1959, was rescheduled for August 24 in Stettler. Police didn't add any new charges as a result of his breakout or the accompanying felonies.

How Cook managed to escape from the hospital cell-block received a great deal of attention. Two contradicting opinions emerged from this investigation. One idea held that someone on the outside had helped Cook escape. The weight of this theory lay in the unusual type of bolts used to secure the windows in the forensic cells. Somehow, the accused man must have sent word to an accomplice detailing the type of wrench he needed to open the window bars, and then this person had supplied him with the tool. This same person (or persons) may also have stolen the car and brought it to Cook. If someone went to all that trouble and risk to set Cook free, why didn't they also bring the man clothing, money, and perhaps some food? And when and how were they able to communicate with Cook and he with them?

The alternative theory held that, during his ten-day stay in the old hospital, Cook had spent much of his time loosening the window bolts. The hospital had been constructed in 1911. In the forty-eight years since, a considerable amount of settling would have occurred in the building. Through this normal process, the bolts securing the windows may have worked themselves loose.

When recaptured, Cook was still wearing hospital-issue pajama bottoms under a pair of stolen pants, but he had substituted women's rain boots for the slippers and managed to add a stolen hat to his attire — far short of the wardrobe of choice for surviving in the bush.

A convincing argument against the accomplice theory is that in order to take advantage of outside assistance he would have needed at least one opportunity to communicate his needs confidentially to someone willing to help him. Being a popular inmate and having been released the same day as many other convicts, it's feasible that he had such connections, but there's no indication that any of his friends came to visit him in Ponoka. Prison guards in the shops at various jails had noted in Cook's file that he showed considerable mechanical ability and was a diligent worker. These qualities combined with the half hour between the guards' patrols and powerful motivation make it reasonable to assume that he acted alone.

Whichever theory authorities subscribed to, no one thought returning Cook to the forensic ward in the aging Ponoka hospital was a good idea, and so until August 24 legal and medical personnel could visit him at "the Fort."

Magistrate G.W. Graves called the preliminary hearing to order just as, only blocks away, the twenty-sixth annual Stettler Flower Show opened. W.F. Macdonald, a lawyer from Red Deer, represented the Crown's interests, and David MacNaughton was joined by well-known criminal lawyer Giffard Main. It was a poorly kept secret that the flamboyant Main, who loved nothing more than a courtroom challenge, provided his services to Cook free of charge.

Main did not disappoint those who chose the crowded and stuffy courtroom over the beauty of floral displays. When, after a lunch recess, the prosecutor's chair fell apart beneath him, Main expressed the hope that the Crown's case would "collapse like that chair."

Later in the afternoon, when the defendant laughed audibly at a response from his friend Jimmy Myhaluk, who was on the witness stand at the time, Crown prosecutor Macdonald took exception.

"The accused seems amused," he noted.

In classic Main-style, the defense attorney countered, "He is entitled to be amused. It is no crime."

The quips provided a bit of badly needed comic-relief to the otherwise gruesome hearing. By Friday, August 28, despite protestations from the defense, Magistrate Graves decreed that the evidence he had heard warranted a trial. He established Red Deer as the venue.

On Monday, November 30, Robert Raymond Cook issued a not-guilty plea to the murder charge read by Mr. Justice Peter Greschuk. Jury selection began immediately. As was the custom of the time, six men were chosen to hear the evidence and ponder the guilt or innocence of the accused. According to court records, jurors W.P. Bolze, L.M. Edgar, Graham Stephens, Harry

Harrison, and M.J. Pixley chose Gerald Wates to represent them as the jury foreman. J. Wallace Anderson replaced Macdonald as the Crown prosecutor, and because of their extensive first-hand knowledge of the case, RCMP officers Joseph Van Blarcom and Thomas Roach assisted the prosecutor. Main continued to represent Cook, with MacNaughton as his assistant.

Constable George Sproule, the first witness, remained on the stand until the court adjourned just before five o'clock that afternoon. Sproule presented technical information about the pieces of evidence accumulated throughout the investigation, as well as the chronology of events. Among the items introduced as exhibits was a small black-and-white photo showing Bob Cook mugging it up with his friend Jimmy Myhaluk. In the photo, Cook wore a tie with a very distinctive pattern, a pattern that appeared to be identical to that on the tie found under the blood-soaked mattress in the Cook's bedroom. If Giffard Main had reservations about this photograph being used as evidence, he remained silent.

A dishevelled-looking Robert Cook is led away, handcuffed to an RCMP officer. (Courtesy of the Glenbow Archives, Calgary.)

When the trial re-convened Tuesday morning, December 1, the balance of Sproule's testimony was postponed. Pathologist Dr. Peter Davey needed to return to his duties in Edmonton and so he took the stand next. In his testimony, he altered his estimate of the time of the Cook family's deaths. At the preliminary hearing, Davey had stated that the deaths occurred between twenty-four and ninety-six hours prior to his examination on Sunday evening.

"I would feel they had been dead more than twenty-four hours because the rigor mortis which sets in just after death had run its course, and the bodies were pliable again. I felt they had been dead less than seventy-two hours because disruption of the internal organs due to gases had not occurred," he amended.

Giffard Main asked the doctor if this meant the Cooks could have been killed at two o'clock Friday morning. Davey confirmed that this was within the parameters.

Peggy Van Der Stoel, a serologist (expert in blood analysis) with the RCMP, took the stand next.

"I understand that you have no method of determining the age of blood stains?" asked defense lawyer Main, during his cross-examination.

The witness confirmed that the lawyer's understanding was correct.

"You ... can't tell if ... any particular [blood] stains were two days old or two months old?"

"No, sir," Van Der Stoel confirmed once again before being excused from the witness stand.

The parade of witnesses — experts and local citizens — continued over the next several days, and this testimony re-created the events leading up to Cook's arrest and the subsequent discovery of the bodies.

Car salesman Len Amoroso took the stand. Crown prosecutor Wallace Anderson's questions made the jurors dramatically aware that Robert Cook showed no hesitation in lying to complete a transaction.

Next, Anderson called Walter Berezowski. The ex-convict and acquaintance of Cook took the stand. Main tried to introduce the gist of a conversation between the witness and the accused — to establish the fact that Cook spoke freely and frequently about the cache of money awaiting him on his release from jail. Giving information about money buried in a town, Bowden, the site of a provincial jail, which many of his fellow prisoners knew well, was surely an open invitation to them to race to the site immediately upon release.

As enlightening as the testimony would have been, Mr. Justice Greschuk refused to allow the conversation to be introduced as evidence. Main argued his point vehemently but without success. Perhaps to establish his displeasure, Main asked the question anyway, but before Berezowski began to answer, Greschuk ruled Main's question out of order and the witness stepped down.

Having just lost what he had hoped was an opportunity to establish the notion that the family might have been killed by any number of former inmates, Main asked that Constable Sproule be recalled. Main wished to discuss the photograph of the accused and his friend Myhaluk. Main reviewed the similarity in design between the tie Cook wore in the photo and that found at the scene of the crime. He then asked what colour the tie in the photo was. As it was a black-and-white picture, no one could know for sure and therefore the assumption that the tie was the same one found later by Sproule was spurious.

From the prisoner's box, Robert Cook appeared to be paying understandably close attention to the proceedings. Dressed in a white shirt, sports jacket, neat trousers, and well-polished brown leather shoes, he bore little resemblance to the exhausted fugitive apprehended four and a half months previously.

An assortment of Stettler citizens testified next. These witnesses established Robert Cook's presence in Stettler on the afternoon and early evening of Thursday, June 25. The accused's clothing during that period was also established. Robert Cook had been wearing the light blue, prison-issue suit, later found hidden in his parents' home, covered in blood. Others testified that the day after they were last seen alive, Raymond and Daisy Cook failed to keep obligations they had arranged and had not mentioned plans of moving to British Columbia.

Mary Sarah Heck testified that she'd seen a white convertible backed up to the garage on Raymond Cook's property early Saturday evening.

John Bell, the Camrose police officer who had contacted Stettler RCMP after hearing the news of the mass murder, described his altercations with the man he knew as "Raymond Cook."

The next witnesses came from considerably farther away. The accountant and the deputy warden of the penitentiary in Prince Albert testified next.

Accountant Pierre Jutras' testimony created more questions than it answered. He explained that when Cook left the prison the morning of Tuesday, June 23, 1959, he had $31.81 with him. Previous witnesses had already established that Cook spent money that day in Saskatoon, the next day in Edmonton, and on Thursday in Stettler. On the Friday he had relinquished a further ninety dollars to Hood Motors as a down payment on the now-impounded Impala convertible. Where did Cook get the additional money? He had maintained that he unearthed his tobacco tin of money from its hiding place in Bowden, continued on to Stettler, and had given his father $4,100 and kept two hundred dollars for himself.

Deputy warden John Weeks explained that Cook's parents wrote to him while he served his time and that their last letter was enclosed in a parcel containing a gift of the shirt, tie, and socks he wore when released. Weeks also shed some light on the April 1st fight in prison, which had left Cook with some thirty stitches in his head. An inmate named Oliver Durocher had started the altercation, and while Cook was hospitalized after the incident, Durocher went to solitary confinement. Weeks related that the general consensus among prisoners and staff was that the savage beating Cook received stemmed from a deeply rooted and still unresolved dispute between the two men. Durocher and Cook were released from jail on the same day.

When Weeks left the witness stand, it was after four o'clock in the afternoon. Mr. Justice Greschuk adjourned court for the day, advising all that it would reconvene the next day, Saturday, for the morning only. Robert Raymond Cook was the first witness called on that unusual weekend sitting. After having his client, rather redundantly, identify himself, Giffard Main asked, "Did you kill your father, Ray Cook?"

"No sir, I certainly didn't," came Cook's firm reply.

Through a series of questions and answers, Cook admitted his long criminal record, but declared that his relationship with his family remained positive. They had kept in touch with him, mostly through letters written by Daisy Cook. Bob Cook, in turn, had written to the folks back in Stettler on a fairly regular basis.

Main also wanted to clarify the situation with Oliver Durocher, the man Cook had fought with while in jail. Cook contended the dispute arose over the operation of the prison's boxing club — an apt topic for a fist fight. Cook further reported that a note from Durocher, smuggled from solitary, expressed Durocher's regret that he had not "finished the job." Oddly, Cook advised the court that the two former antagonists, however, peacefully quaffed a pint or two together in a Saskatoon bar the day of their combined releases. This testimony set the tone for the balance of Cook's stay in the witness stand. Cook presented an image of himself as a loving and dutiful son who helped his family realize their dreams. Sure he lived away from home much of the time, but that couldn't be considered too unusual; after all he was an adult and had long ago finished his schooling. What was left unmentioned was that his residences, while not living at home, were various jail cells, and that his method of acquiring funds to assist his family were not legal.

Cook went on to explain this lifestyle had led to behaviours that those who'd never served time might find peculiar. For instance, one never gives an honest answer to the police. Hence, when they questioned him, Cook lied, even about the clothes he'd been wearing. He explained that from his cell beneath the Stettler police station he'd overheard comments about a blue suit found at the scene of the crime and he was afraid to associate himself with it.

"I was scared ... it's kind of hard to explain, but if you've been in a few mix-ups with the police it's just about natural, the first rule is never tell the truth. You just lie. I don't know. You just don't tell the truth, that's all."

It's interesting that Main chose to reveal his client as a liar.

Cook then described leaving the $4,100 with his parents and offering his father the suit he'd been given when he left prison. In return, Raymond Cook had given his son the keys to the family's 1958 station wagon and permission to "trade it off" on a vehicle of his son's choice. Robert Cook added that his father had also given him his wallet with the car ownership and all of Raymond Cook's identification in it. The younger Cook explained that they both thought using the elder Cook's identification instead of his own would make the transaction simpler.

Thus equipped, Cook related that he left Stettler about 10:30 that evening and arrived in Edmonton roughly two hours later. While cruising hotels and bars, he met several of his friends from jail. Cook remembered having coffee with former inmate Jack Mitchell before meeting up with his old chum from the reformatory, Sonny Wilson. Cook explained, with little coaxing from his attorney, that Wilson was planning a break-in but his accomplices had not shown up. The accused volunteered his services in their stead. He described the misadventure in great detail, the detail of a man who'd been there. He knew the layout of the dry-cleaning establishment they burglarized and the amount and type of loot they absconded with. Police records confirmed that the break-in had occurred, the business-owner testified later that Bob's description of the missing possessions were accurate.

This testimony indicated that Bob Cook might well have been over one hundred miles away from Stettler during the first of the time period in which the pathologist had stated the murders had taken place. At that point, court was adjourned for the balance of the weekend. The next week, both Sonny Wilson and Jack Mitchell, testified confirming Cook's words. Both statements were noteworthy: Wilson's because it was an admission of guilt in connection with a crime he hadn't been charged with, and Mitchell's because his testimony showed that he and many other inmates knew of Cook's father's plan to give Bob the family station wagon and of the amount and location of Bob's stash of money.

Crown prosecutor Anderson questioned the accused next. He clearly didn't believe Cook's story about the money hidden in Bowden, so he asked Cook to review the sequence of events from the day after his release to his arrest on false pretense charges. When Cook indicated that he had dug the money up and then partied in several Edmonton hotels, bars, and motels, Anderson expressed surprise that none of his friends noticed the thick wad of bills in his pocket. Cook merely shrugged as Anderson put this opinion in a general way to the court, not as a specific question to the accused. Giffard Main reacted to his learned colleague's presumption by scribbling madly on a pad of paper.

Next, Anderson began to point out differences in Cook's story about the break-in with Sonny Wilson's description. Curiously, Cook conceded that because it was dark in the dry-cleaning store he might be confused about the number of staircases he scaled during the burglary.

Perhaps encouraged by this rather odd statement, Anderson headed full force into attacking Cook's credibility. He reminded the court of Bob's admitted deceit when dealing with the police, of the lies told to the car salesman, and other instances where the accused's statements had created considerable credibility gaps.

In his re-examination, Giffard Main vainly attempted to rescue his client's image.

Crown prosecutor Anderson's summation began and ended the next morning. His points hinged on Cook's only alibi — burglarizing the dry cleaners at the probable time of the murderers. This had not even been brought forward until more than five months after police laid the murder charge. Anderson suggested this made the alibi suspect.

The next day, Main spent a further six hours summing up the case for the jury. As Bob Cook suspected right from his first days in the Stettler RCMP cells, the blue prison-issue suit proved to be an important article.

" ... the reason that the suit was hidden beneath the mattress was not to hide the fact that it was Bob Cook's suit, but to hide the fact that there were bloodstains on it. Whoever did this job was afraid of an early discovery of the tragedy, and he wanted time to get away. Now if the prisoner, Bob Cook, had done this awful thing, his concealment of the suit under the mattress wouldn't have affected him one iota," the seasoned defense attorney proposed.

He further theorized that the murderer hadn't been wearing that much-debated pale blue suit. Instead, Ray Cook was either wearing it when he was killed by person or persons unknown, or he had taken it off and hung it on the bed post before going to bed. And this was where, Main explained, the suit had become splattered with blood.

Next, Main called upon his assistant, David MacNaughton, to stand up, turn his back to the jurors and lift his black robes. While MacNaughton held that peculiar pose, Main reminded the court of Anderson's doubt that Cook could have carried over $4,000 in his pockets, undetected. The jury gazed upon MacNaughton's back pockets as he carefully removed two wads of money, totaling $4,300.

Concluding his summation, Main harshly criticized the police for what he felt was an investigation full of neglect. He implied that because they immediately assumed Robert Cook murdered his family, they didn't follow up any leads that might have proved otherwise. Main readily conceded that his client had a lengthy criminal record, but he reminded the court that not only should this fact not serve to condemn the young man but it actually spoke in his favour. After all, in all the crimes Robert Raymond Cook committed, he had never shown violent tendencies.

Mr. Justice Greschuk ordered a recess and advised all concerned that his address to the jury would be lengthy. He kept his word. For five hours, he addressed such important issues for consideration as circumstantial evidence, technical evidence, the premise of reasonable doubt, in addition to giving a summary of all the testimony given during the trial.

He then ordered the jury to deliberate. An hour and a half later, the foreman announced that they'd reached a decision and that the decision was "guilty as charged." Justice Greschuk then asked, in a voice still hoarse from his five-hour dissertation, "Robert Cook, have you anything to say?"

"All I have to say, sir, is that I am not guilty; I couldn't have done this, and I didn't do it."

A hush fell over the courtroom.

"You shall be returned to the cells in Fort Saskatchewan. On April 15, 1960, you shall be taken from that place and hanged. May God have mercy on your soul."

The next day, Friday, December 11, Giffard Main announced his intention to seek a re-trial. While he did so, a prison-appointed psychiatrist examined Robert Cook, as were all convicts awaiting execution. Dr. L.E. Cathcart later reported that Cook clearly did not relate well to people, nor did people make much of an impact on him. He explained that he barely remembered his natural mother and that his descriptions of his father and stepmother were "two-dimensional." He did not mention any of his five siblings. In somewhat of a contradiction to this, Cook told the doctor that he'd broken out of Ponoka mental hospital because he wanted to attend his family's funeral.

Cathcart wrote in his official report: "He still insists that he is not guilty, and he certainly acts the part. At most times the prisoner seems to act like a wholesome kid, particularly when he is discussing music and singing, [and] has several favourites on the radio. It's getting harder and harder to see this fellow a wholesale murderer of his own folks."

In Cathcart's professional opinion, "Robert Cook was quite sane."

On April 6, the RCMP received information from an inspector with the Vancouver police force. It concerned the Cook murder case and came to him via "a usually reliable source." The facts he'd become aware of pointed strongly to the possibility that Oliver Durocher, Cook's assailant in the prison boxing-club-related fight, had murdered the Stettler family. When scrutinized, the story was not as reliable as it had first seemed. Durocher could account for his whereabouts during the hours in question, and the person who supposedly saw him in the area around the time of the murder couldn't have — he was in a jail cell just outside Calgary during the last week of June 1959.

Giffard Main's efforts to arrange a new trial for Robert Cook's were rewarded. He maintained that some of the comments that had passed between his client and the police should not have been admitted as evidence. On Monday, June 20, 1960, Robert Cook's appeal trial opened. Mr. Justice Harold Riley took the bench; Anderson continued as Crown prosecutor; and Giffard Main's partner, Frank Dunne, and David MacNaughton represented the accused. To his great disappointment, Main's health didn't allow him to continue acting on behalf of the defendant. Again a six-man jury would listen to and assess the evidence.

Unlike most re-trials, which are usually based on careful legal manoeuvers rather than on additional information and surprise witnesses, Cook's second rivaled a Perry Mason courtroom scene for drama and suspense.

Crown prosecutor Anderson called the first new witness. Mavis Dawes lived on 52 Street in Stettler, just a few houses from the Cook family's home. Just before this second trial, another neighbour of the Dawes's, Sergeant Tom Roach, approached her and asked if she remembered hearing anything unusual the night the murders were thought to have taken place. She did indeed; the woman distinctly remembered hearing two gunshots around midnight on June 25, 1959. Although she admitted on the witness stand that the sounds she heard might actually have been that of a car or truck backfiring, she later scoffed at that suggestion.

"I've been around firearms all my life, I couldn't be mistaken about what they sound like," Mavis Dawes protested.

What she heard was one thing the prosecution feared might be viewed with some reservation; the other was the fact that Mrs. Dawes hadn't come forward to report what she'd heard until encouraged to do so by the town cop almost exactly a year later.

Robert McAlister took the stand next. He had sold Raymond Cook the family station wagon, which Robert later traded in on the much flashier Impala convertible. His testimony indicated that Raymond Cook had chosen that particular car carefully and had frequently commented on how it suited his purposes. As Cook had purchased the car less than a year before, and his requirements for a vehicle hadn't changed in the elapsed time, McAlister deemed it very unlikely that Ray Cook would be anxious to sign the car over to his son.

Next, a young woman named Gail Smith took the stand. She identified herself as a friend of Jimmy Myhaluk's and explained that she'd been at the Myhaluk's home visiting with Jim on Wednesday, June 24. During the evening, Smith remembered Robert Cook dropping in. Apparently the suit he'd been wearing when he left Prince Albert the day before had since become wet from a rain storm. Smith confirmed that she recalled this clearly because she offered to press the suit for Jim's friend. The young woman also related to the court that Bob spoke of going to Stettler to pick up a station wagon.

Robert Cook had returned to the Myhaluk home, Smith explained, driving a station wagon and wearing different clothes. Mrs. Myhaluk, Jimmy's mother, had asked Cook what happened to his suit. He replied that he had ripped it.

The next witness proved that, even when he wasn't present, Giffard Main could make an impression in a courtroom. Margery Constance Main, Mrs. Giffard Main, took the stand. She testified that she received an anonymous phone call for her husband. The caller had left the following message: "You tell your husband to lay off the Cook case. He is not to get Cook off. Cook has got to go."

The caller also threatened to harm her and the couple's three children if Cook went free.

In a final attempt to save his client's life, defense lawyer Frank Dunne asked that the jurors be excused while he presented what he felt was a contentious point of law.

"The Richler case in the Supreme Court of Canada lays down that where the accused gives an explanation which might reasonably be true, not which is believed, but which might reasonably be true, he is entitled to be acquitted."

Dunne pointed out to Justice Riley that not only had the accused maintained he was nowhere near the scene of the murder during the hours in question but that the court had heard his alibi backed up by both Sonny Wilson and Jack Mitchell. Three people claimed that when Mavis Dawes heard the two lethal shots at 12:10 a.m. on Friday, June 26, Bob Cook was nowhere near the scene of the crime. Dunne also suggested that, since all the evidence the Crown presented was circumstantial in nature, His Lordship would be well advised to direct the jury toward an acquittal.

The judge denied both requests and the jury returned to hear the balance of the evidence.

Frank Dunne's summation suggested that his client had absolutely no motive for murdering his family, that Raymond Cook had apparently agreed to give Bob the family car upon his release. Further, if Cook had worn the blue suit while murdering his family he would not have left it in such a conspicuous spot. Finally, Dunne protested that there was little likelihood that any one person had murdered all seven people single-handedly. Whoever murdered the Cooks had help, Dunne insisted. With as many as sixty prisoners being released on the same day, many with a knowledge of Robert Cook's stash, the murder could have been committed by any number of persons.

The Crown protested that Robert Cook did, indeed, have a motive for killing his family. His family's apparently clandestine plans to move to British Columbia had infuriated him. Cook realized that it was only his unexpectedly early release from jail and arrival home that had interfered with their successful attempt to permanently sever all ties with him. Anderson theorized that on the evening of Thursday, June 25, 1959, Bob Cook had either not left his parents home at 10:30 as he claimed or only left briefly and returned once he knew his family would be asleep and therefore more vulnerable to his murderous rage. Cook had worked through the night concealing the bodies and cleaning some of the mess. Anderson further expounded that Cook left the home for a time around day-break Friday, intending to return and finish cleaning. He did return, Saturday evening, but finding the crime had so far gone undetected he left again, secure in his hot new car and the incorrect assumption that he'd gotten away with murders — seven of them.

Mr. Justice Harold Riley took only forty-five minutes to review, for the jury, the material presented during the trial which had begun nine days before. His summation weighed heavily on the side of the prosecution and included the remarks: "My own concluding observation is simply this: that the key to this whole foul affair may well be found in the blue suit... The conclusion is almost inescapable that the person who was wearing that suit and who placed it under the mattress was the person who did the killing. That is a mere expression of opinion on my part and it is in no way binding on you, and you, of course, have the paramount right to disagree with me. The weight of the evidence means there are only two possible verdicts: guilty of murder or acquittal."

After hearing over a quarter of a million words of testimony and taking something over half an hour to reflect upon these words and their implications, the jury foreman, well-respected Edmonton businessman Henry Singer, announced that the jury had reached an unanimous decision on their first ballot. Robert Cook, they believed, was guilty as charged.

Once again Cook heard a date for his hanging established and the horrific words, "May God have mercy on your soul."

The defense appealed the ruling, citing Mr. Justice Riley's direction to the jury regarding Cook's alibi for the hours in which the killings took place. Five Supreme Court judges debated the contention. Four felt that justice had been done and the fifth voted for a new trial.

Robert Cook himself began to take an active role in preserving his life. He wrote to the solicitor general, protesting his innocence. Even then-Prime Minister John Diefenbaker listened sympathetically to the doomed man's plight and suggested, in cabinet, on November 14, 1960, that Cook might be innocent. Just hours later, the lifeless body of Robert Raymond Cook hung at the end of a rope in the basement of the Fort Saskatchewan jail.

The "old" Fort Saskatchewan jail where Robert Cook was held and then hanged. He was the last person ever put to death in that institution and in Alberta. (Photo by Robert Smith.)

Little is known now that was not known then, but academics and ordinary folk alike have delved into the case, each finding evidence to support one premise or the other. Neil Boyd, director of the Criminology Research Centre at Simon Fraser University in British Columbia, includes the case in his book *The Last Dance: Murder in Canada.* He summed up the results of his research this way: "Who killed the Cook family? Possibly someone just out of Prince Albert [penitentiary], possibly someone from closer to home, but don't put any money on Bobby Cook. He was a thief and a break-and-enter specialist, but it's unlikely that he was a murderer." [1]

In the book *The Robert Cook Murder Case* by Frank Anderson, the epilogue consists of a 1978 interview with Sonny Wilson, who maintains he was in Edmonton with Cook during the time of the murders. Wilson was asked, "Why do you think Cook did it?" with the apparent intention of eliciting an outburst of protestation about his deceased friend's innocence. Wilson merely replied, "I never pass judgment on my fellow man." [2]

Many who have not formally studied or written about the case are still interested in passing comment on it. A half sister of Ray Cook's implies that the family hoped to move to British Columbia while Bob finished serving his time in order to escape the constant stress that the young man's lawbreaking created in their home.

This premise may be contradicted by facts uncovered while sorting out Ray and Daisy Cook's estate. As noted in Brian Swarbrick's series of features in the *Edmonton Sun* from Sunday, February 26, to Sunday, March 4, 1984, Ray Cook's bank balance stood at $3,664.84 (more than $20,000 by today's standards) and there had been no activity on the account for over four months. In addition, Cook owned his home outright, a truck, and a very nearly new car, and comfortably supported a wife and five dependent children on his wages as a mechanic. Could Ray have actually been on the receiving end of some of his son's booty? [3]

When relatives began the unpleasant chore of clearing the Cook family's possessions from their home in order to sell it and settle the estate, "half the tools missing from Modern Machine Shop where Ray worked turned up in the Cook basement." These finds, coupled with a considerably larger-than-expected savings fund, could indicate Robert Cook came by his dishonest ways honestly. [4]

The new owner of the property at 5018 52 Street, Stettler, Alberta, decided his real-estate needs would be better served by tearing down the Cook's green-and-white clapboard bungalow and putting up a small apartment building. During the demolition and excavation, no trace of the $4,100 Robert Cook claimed he left on the kitchen table turned up. In a strange, and rather morbid, twist of fate, Mavis Dawes, whose evidence at the second trial became the defining words about when the murders actually occurred, moved into the newly built apartment house. Her suite is in the basement, with its living room in the same spot as the grease-pit-cum-makeshift-grave.[5]

Although the damaged shotgun was identified as the murder weapon early in the investigation, who owned it and how it came to be at the scene of the crime remains a mystery.

Was Cook hanged because he murdered his family or was he hanged because his protestations of innocence weren't believed in the wake of his chronic lying and lawbreaking. No one can ever say for sure. What can be said now, with accuracy, is that Robert Cook became the last man hanged in Alberta.

What a difference the passage of years has made to sentencing. On August 6, 1991, thirty-two years after twenty-two-year-old Robert Cook may have murdered his family, fifteen-year-old Gavin Mandin killed his mother, stepfather and two younger sisters. The murders took place at the family's hobby farm near Valleyview, Alberta.

That morning the four had gone into town grocery shopping. Gavin stayed behind. He waited in the three-room shack, which served as the family's residence during stays at the vacation property, armed with a .22 pump-action rifle. As he saw the car pull up near the house, the youngster fired at his stepfather, Maurice's head, killing the man instantly. Next he shot his mother in the chest, and explained afterward that he then felt obliged to kill his sisters.

He pushed his 220-pound stepfather's body out of the car and drove into the bush in an attempt to hide the three bodies. Before abandoning the car and its grisly contents, he cut his mother's dress open to expose her breasts and genitals. Gavin later explained he wanted to see what a breast looked like. Next, he tied his stepfather's body to an all-terrain vehicle and towed it into the woods. Having disposed of the bodies, he returned to the cabin where, for two days, he debated what to do. At times the idea of suicide seemed appealing; at others he felt that calling the police would be the best move. In the end he decided to escape in the family's mini-van.

The RCMP first noticed the van being driven well below the speed limit in the town of Whitecourt. When they tried to approach it to question the driver, the van sped off and a high-speed chase ensued. Gavin Mandin was arrested minutes later near the town of Mayerthorpe, when a spike belt placed across the road disabled his vehicle.

In a routine attempt to contact the youth's parents, police discovered the murders. They charged Gavin with four counts of first-degree murder and ordered him to Alberta Hospital for a psychiatric assessment.

The quiet teen explained that he was angry with his parents because he was fed up with doing chores. He further complained that his mother never had time to listen to him and that he resented the fact that discipline was a "do as I say, not as I do" arrangement in his home.

The examining psychologist diagnosed Gavin as "psychotic," a term the lad did not enjoy having pinned on him. He's more comfortable with telling people about his I.Q. of 133 — near-genius level.

Gavin Mandin was first ordered to stand trial in adult court; however, because he was only fifteen when he committed the crimes, the decision was overturned and the case was scheduled for youth court. In November, 1993, that decision was reversed and he was back in adult court. The Supreme Court of Canada upheld the ruling, and Gavin Mandin came before Edmonton's Court of Queen's Bench and Justice Eileen Nash on Valentine's Day, 1994. Exactly a month later, the eighteen year old received the stiffest sentence possible — life. Because he had already served two and a half years while waiting for the ruling, he will be eligible for parole in the year 2001.

THE FAT LADY SINGS

Marguerite Pitre always dreaded the oppressive heat that summer brought to her beloved Quebec City. She felt greatly relieved when Labour Day came, heralding a return to more moderate temperatures. Marguerite's obesity had become a constant inconvenience, but in the summer this burden verged on unbearable. Much in this woman's life displeased her but, oddly, she didn't view any of these vexations as her responsibility to rectify. They were merely cards that fate had dealt her.

In addition to the enormity of her body and its attendant drawbacks, Marguerite, a widow, was chronically short of funds. As a waitress she barely made enough money to scrape through, day to day. Despite her best efforts there was never anything left over from any of her pay cheques. This fiscal tension was worsened by an old debt to a man she had worked with in a munitions factory during the war. Albert Guay hadn't pressured Marguerite for repayment. Even so, the situation concerned her: it was now 1949, the debt was several years old, and her financial situation showed no signs of improving.

Guay rarely gave the debt a thought. Once the war ended he had been able to leave his job in the munitions factory and concentrate on his jewellery business. His friendship with the heavy-set Marguerite continued, and he had hired her brother, Genereux Ruest, as his watchmaker. This arrangement went beyond merely business because, although a highly skilled tradesman, the fifty-two-year-old Ruest was almost unemployable. In today's politically correct lingo, Ruest would be described as "profoundly physically challenged." His less enlightened, post-war society simply referred to him as "a cripple." Medically, the man's affliction was termed "tubercular paralytic."

Had Guay not employed Genereux, the widow Pitre's meager funds might have had to stretch further to include her brother's care.

Although Marguerite felt grateful to Guay, the situation also made her feel uncomfortable: a proud woman, she found the long-standing debt offensive. For this reason she listened intently when Guay telephoned her in late June 1949 and asked that they meet to discuss a plan.

"Come to the shop at lunch next Friday," Guay urged.

Marguerite agreed.

Closed blinds darkened the St. Sauveur Street store windows, the Open/Closed sign twisted to indicate the latter. This didn't surprise Pitre; lunch-hour closings were the norm. Despite this, and also in keeping with the time and place, Guay's shop door remained unlocked. Marguerite let herself in. Both Guay and Marguerite's brother, Genereux, greeted her warmly.

Knowing that the brother and sister would have to return to their regular work in less than an hour, Albert Guay came directly to the point of the meeting he'd arranged.

"Marguerite, I know you're self-conscious about your debt to me, and I want to make arrangements today to clear that off."

"I have no extra money just now. Perhaps in a few weeks. I'll try, Albert," the woman explained revealing her discomfort about the state of affairs.

"Don't worry, Marguerite. I realize your position, but it's not money I'm after. That's why I've asked you both here today. I need your help," Guay said. "If you can see your way clear to helping me with this project, we'll just forget about the debt."

Genereux Ruest looked as relieved as his sister did. His wages were not nearly enough for him to help Marguerite honour her obligations. A falling out between these two able bodied people, so significant in his life, could mean the end of Genereux's career as Albert Guay's watchmaker. Shivers ran up the man's grotesquely deformed spine just thinking of the dreadful existence he'd be doomed to, living on the government's meager stipend for cripples.

The jewellery shop owner asked only one favour of each of the siblings: that Genereux apply his watchmaking skills toward the construction of a time-keeping device, and that Marguerite deliver a parcel to the city's airport.

They struck agreement in short order, and the three continued about their daily business. Genereux's backlog of watches for repair demanded his attention. Marguerite could waste no time catching the trolley to her job at a downtown restaurant. Management took a dim view of employees arriving late for their shifts.

Albert, however, decided to take the afternoon off. He wanted to visit a friend. The pretty Marie Ange Robitaille was good for him. (The press variously listed the young woman's age, in 1949, somewhere between sixteen and twenty-six.) Albert had been distressed when, a few weeks before, a violent misunderstanding flared between the two. Angrily, Marie accused Albert of making no effort to leave his wife. Embarrassingly, police had been called. They laid a charge of "threatening" against Albert and fined him $25.

The incident brought Guay to an ugly realization: his marriage was a sham. Despite being an adequate mother to his four-year-old daughter, his wife, Rita, was not only demanding but decidedly unexciting. Besides, she greatly interfered with the pursuit of his love affair.

"Either you leave your wife or I leave you," Marie had declared, not allowing much room for negotiation.

In hindsight, Guay knew he shouldn't have pulled the revolver from his pocket. He had panicked: he only wanted to silence Marie, but his actions had terrified her. Still, though, her call to the police had been unnecessary. After all, he had explained over and over again to Marie that he would look after his marital status in his own way and on his own schedule.

This incident, however, forced Albert's hand. He had to act or he would lose Marie, a thought he couldn't bear. There was always the chance, too, that Marie would pay a visit to the Guay home as she'd threatened more than once. If the two women spoke to one another, Albert Guay's future would lie in tatters at his wife's feet.

Rita Guay remained blissfully unaware of her husband's extra-marital activities. Had she even a suspicion, her strict Roman Catholic background and her self-righteousness would spell lifelong misery for Albert.

Guay knew he could no longer afford the luxury of procrastination. And so, having determined his plan, he looked forward to a well-earned afternoon of lovemaking. He left the shop, flagged a cab, gave the driver Marie's address, and rehearsed a marriage proposal.

Guay's impromptu visit took the young woman completely by surprise. Marie stared blankly at her lover standing in the grimy hallway, but before she had time to invite him in, Albert took her hand, looked into her eyes, and with a resolution motivated by fear and lust rather than love and a sense of the romantic, blurted out: "By the end of the year we'll be married. We'll bring in the new decade together. You mark my words."

The two then spent an energetic and satisfying afternoon together.

E.T. Stannard, R.J. Parker and Arthur D. Storke also met that afternoon but in New York City. Just days before, Storke had been named successor to Stannard as president of Kennecott Copper Corporation. Parker held the post of vice president.

Geologists with this firm had recently discovered substantial deposits of titanium ore in rural Quebec. The uses for titanium had been growing rapidly; prosperity awaited any company controlling its supply and distribution.

Initial geological reports indicated that this find was the largest field of titanium in the western hemisphere. Kennecott, already the leading copper producer in North America, looked forward to exploiting this additional resource. The three executives knew their company could shift the world's chief source of supply of titanium from India to their corporate holdings.

Kennecott Corporation valued the find so highly that Stannard, Storke, and Parker's meeting included making plans for a site inspection. And so it was that on September 9, 1949, the high-powered trio, sporting requisite fedoras and briefcases, arrived at Montreal. Here the men boarded a Canadian Pacific Airlines DC-3 for the final leg of their journey, which included a scheduled stop in Quebec City.

The trip was a routine one, and the flight crew quipped lightheartedly with one another as they waited on the runway of Quebec City's Ancienne Airport. Baggage handlers loaded mail and parcels into the belly of the plane while seven additional passengers settled themselves above.

Captain Pierre Laurin was an experienced pilot with seven years and many hours of flying time to his credit. Laurin's co-pilot, Gordon Alexander, had virtually grown up flying. Although only twenty-nine years of age, Alexander had already logged over four thousand hours. Flight Engineer Emile Therrien and Gertrude McKay, the flight attendant, completed the crew roster.

Advised by McKay that all the new and remaining passengers had settled, Laurin waited to hear from Therrien that the additional cargo had been secured. Willie Lamond, a freight handler at the airport, carried a last-minute package out to the aircraft. Just moments before, an obese woman, dressed all in black had placed the parcel on his counter.

"Young man," Marguerite Pitre had panted, out of breath from hurrying with the box, "it is imperative that this parcel be on the flight to Baie Comeau."

Lamond looked momentarily confused. He knew pilots hated being kept waiting and that the plane was ready for take-off, but revealing the naive mindset of those post-war days and risking the wrath of the flight crew, Lamond complied.

Moments later the DC-3 taxied to its final take-off.

With the crew and the mine-company executives that day were three children, seven men and six women. Fate and the twisted minds of three people were about to tie these twenty-three lives, and deaths, together forever in Canadian criminal history.

Oscar Tremblay, a section man for Canadian National Railways, looked up from his work along a strip of track near St. Joachim, about forty miles east of Quebec City.

"I was near four other fellows working along the tracks when I heard some sort of explosion," he explained. "I looked up and saw this big plane suddenly turn and head for the hills north of the railway line. It struck a big cape [Cape Tourmente rises at a steep angle from the shore of the St. Lawrence River] ... on the inland side of the railway. I called to the other men. We were sure the plane had fallen not far away and we went through the bush and saw the wreckage.

"It was the most awful scene I have ever come across. There were arms and legs and even heads torn from the bodies. There were mangled bodies of little children. Pieces of the plane were scattered all about the bush. We thought we would find the plane in flames but we didn't. There was no fire at all, just a mass of wreckage and all those bodies."

Still badly shaken by the horror of what he and his workmates saw, Tremblay concluded, "There was nothing we could do so we came out of the bush and reported to the railway, but I'll never forget that sight as long as I live." [1]

Tremblay's employers immediately radioed word of the horrific tragedy and assembled a special four-car rescue train. Sadly, the urgency was futile. Would-be rescuers found the only job left to them was that of pallbearers. They readily recovered all but two bodies.

While workers loaded corpses onto the hastily prepared coaches, representatives from the Department of Transport, Canadian Pacific Airlines, insurance companies and police combed the isolated site. Railway employees witnessing the tragedy answered repetitive questions. All agreed an explosion had precipitated the crash. That wasn't much of a clue, but for now it was all investigators had — that and the fact that the crash had defied every law of physics: "the huge fuel tanks on the wrecked plane did not explode." [2]

The onerous investigation into the crash began. Hastily prepared shuttle trains made their way to Sault Au Cochon, a flag stop some sixteen miles from the village of St. Joachim. At that point a railway scooter took investigators to within a mile of the crash scene. From there the thick forest prohibited exploration by any except those experienced on timber trails.

Journalists made valiant attempts to capture the essence of the event for their readers and listeners. A photographer tried twice to fly in by private plane before begging officials to be allowed to ride the railway scooter. They denied his request. As the only possible source of transportation to the isolated crash scene it was being reserved for police and others in authority. Considering the magnitude of the destruction, anyone spared exposure to the grim scene should have been thankful.

Despite this, the reporters persisted. A journalist's mandate is clear: bring the news to the people. The photographers showed particular tenacity. Some attempted to walk into the site from the main road, but the five miles of dense bush soon forced them to turn back.

Another group rented a boat on the St. Lawrence River. The Montreal *Gazette* reported, "Their plan was an attempt to walk through the muddy shore and then climb the cliffs into the bush. They haven't been seen since."[3] Presumably they eventually returned by whatever means, without having gained the photos they wanted so desperately. The newspapers resorted to carrying copies of family photographs borrowed from the victims' next of kin. The reporter responsible for commandeering the snapshot of Flight Engineer Emile Therrien pulled off a real coup. He came away with a photo perfectly tailored to evoke readers' emotions. In a picture taken the previous Christmas, Therrien and his wife, Reine, stood proudly behind their two identically dressed, freshly scrubbed sons: Pierre, age five, and Michel, age four. Each child held a toy airplane.

Therrien's body was the last to be recovered in the wreckage. The force of the crash had jammed the crews' bodies into the nose of the aircraft. The impact with the hillside crumpled the plane like so much discarded paper. Therrien's body had been virtually welded into the remains of the DC-3.

By that nightfall, twenty-two bodies had been recovered. The flight manifest confirmed that twenty-three people had been on board.

An executive with the Quebec North Shore Paper Company came forward. Shaking with relief Tarrence Flahiff explained, "Mine may be the last body you're searching for. I was on that flight but my wife persuaded me to get off when it landed in Quebec City."

Sadly, that didn't solve the mystery. Passenger Henri Paul Bouchard's body must have landed in the St. Lawrence River. Three days later it floated to the surface thereby accounting for all twenty-three victims of the second worst air disaster in Canadian history.

But what had precipitated the tragedy? Because the plane hadn't ignited when it crashed, the physical clues were scattered throughout the forest. Investigators started to work immediately. Eye witnesses to the crash were unanimous: they had heard an explosion and had seen a box fall from the plane just before the wreckage plummeted to the ground.

Eel fisherman Patrice Simard retrieved the box and handed it over to authorities.

Specialists inspecting the debris found the plane's ignition switches in the "on" position. The discovery told them that Captain Pierre Laurin had not had any warning of the disaster. Pilot training emphasized that the ignition be shut off if the pilot suspected a crash was imminent. An officer with the experience and credentials of Captain Laurin would, most assuredly, have followed training drills, knowing that doing so could save his passengers, crew and himself from a fatal fire.

Workmen brought as much hard evidence as possible out of the wooded crash site, and coroner Paul Marceau scheduled an inquest to begin on September 15, 1949, in Quebec City.

The metal box that witnesses had seen drop from the plane seconds before the crash underwent a thorough examination in police laboratories. The box contained remnants of a sophisticated and powerful time bomb. Investigators advised Canadian Pacific Airlines that their DC-3 aircraft had been carrying a massively destructive weapon.

Police questioned airline employees about any passengers, luggage or parcels associated with that fateful flight, which might have seemed at all out of the ordinary. As well, the search widened to include CPA's employee records and the DC-3's passenger manifest. They sought anyone connected with the flight or the airline who might have been construed as having a questionable agenda.

Their probings revealed surprisingly little. Not only did they not unearth any employee or former employee with a dangerous grudge, but even the passenger list provided little to pique their trained senses. They discovered only one tenuous anomaly. Police records indicated that a J. Albert Guay, widower of passenger Rita Guay, had been convicted on a charge of threatening and unlawful use of a firearm. The incident had taken place just three months before the plane crash and involved a young waitress named Marie Ange Robitaille. It wasn't a strong lead but it was all they had.

And so authorities paid Mademoiselle Robitaille a visit. Their arrival took the young woman by as much surprise as had Albert's unexpected appearance in early June.

"We need to talk to you awhile, miss," explained one of the officers assigned to the call.

"Then you'd better not be standing out in the hallway," the young Robitaille urged. She didn't want her landlady catching sight of four men at her door, especially as two of them were in police uniforms.

With that invitation, a representative from each of the RCMP, the Quebec Provincial Police, the airlines and the insurance company entered the waitress's sparsely furnished flat. Holding their hats and looking distinctly uncomfortable, the men began to explain their mission more fully.

"Do you know a man named Albert Guay?"

"Yes, I do," she replied.

"What is your relationship with M. Guay?"

"He's a friend. We're friends with each other."

"Mademoiselle, our records indicate that M. Guay was charged by the city police after you called their offices. He drew a gun and threatened you, is that right?"

"Well, yes, we did have a disagreement one day but that's all been mended long ago. We're friends again now."

"I see," the officer concluded.

"Mademoiselle," a second man began, "I want to describe someone to you. Please tell us if this person is anything like someone your friend M. Guay might be associated with."

"All right," the waitress replied, visibly relaxing now with the realization she herself was not the object of their scrutiny.

"It's a middle-aged woman, heavy set who is partial to black clothing."

"Oh, yes, I know who that'd be," Marie brightened, enjoying a new-found sense of importance. "That's Albert's friend Marguerite. I've met her. She always wears black clothes. It's a slimming colour, you know, and well, Marguerite's very fat. Her brother works at Albert's shop. He's a watchmaker and a very skillful one, I understand. Yes, there's no question. If you're looking for a fat, middle-aged woman who wears black and knows Albert, it could only be Marguerite Pitre."

The men thanked Marie Ange and assured her she'd been of valuable assistance. Their next moves were straightforward. They needed warrants for the arrest of J. Albert Guay and Marguerite Morel Pitre.

Local reporters were hot on the heels of the investigators. Although the police weren't ready to reveal a lot, tenacious snooping by the reporters produced some ideas of the progress being made. Details and corrections could come later. For now, the news hounds had amassed enough information to print the following headline and sub-headline on Saturday, September 24, 1949: "Woman Admits Placing Mystery Box on Plane" and "J.A. Guay, Husband of One of the Victims, and Mrs. Arthur Pitre Held by Provincial Police; Third Witness, 'Pretty Waitress' Also Questioned."[4]

Some details were known as fact. J.A. Guay's wife had been aboard the death flight. A recently purchased insurance policy on her life promised $10,000 to the beneficiary. The story apparently involved a love triangle between Guay, his wife, and either the widow, Mrs. Arthur (Marguerite) Pitre, or the 'pretty waitress.'[5]

From there details became hazy. The press reported that police held both Albert Guay and a "drug-dazed mystery woman" in connection with the September 9 plane crash.[6]

Police had picked Marguerite up from work and driven her to the police station for questioning. She was a well-known figure in Quebec city. Her slightly eccentric taste in fashion — she only wore black — had earned her the nicknames "crow" or "raven."

Willie Lamond, baggage handler at Ancienne Airport, positively identified Pitre's picture.

"Yes, that's her," he confirmed without hesitation. "That's the woman who brought the parcel at the last minute. She said it had to get on. She was all out of breath from hurrying and carrying the box. It was addressed to someone in Baie Comeau. I remember her well because I rushed out to the runway and loaded the box on the plane myself."

Lamond's statements complemented Pitre's. When questioned earlier in the day she'd made no attempt to deny delivering the lethal package, but staunchly maintained she knew nothing of any bomb.

"He told me it was a statue and that he was giving it to a friend as a gift," Marguerite explained.

"Who is 'he'?" the officer inquired.

"Why Albert. Albert Guay."

Realizing, perhaps for the first time, the horrendous tragedy she'd been a part of, Marguerite lifted herself from the chair and slowly, shakily, made her way out of the police station. Unable to deal with the situation she'd helped to create, Marguerite Pitre went directly home.

Crown prosecutor Noel Dorion officially pressed a murder charge against Guay, and he referred to a fatal bombing of a Philippines Airlines plane just four months before. Murder charges there pended against one woman and five men. "Guay copied this fiendish plan to the letter."7 The earlier incident also involved a love triangle.

When he'd purchased his wife's ticket on the flight to Baie Comeau, Albert Guay stopped at a vending machine in the airport. He deposited two quarters and within seconds a life insurance policy dropped from the machine ensuring that his wife's death would be a fiscally rewarding event.

"Knowing the way in which this diabolical scheme was conceived may not be of tremendous value to our case. But it does help to clear up matters a bit, and it may be of help in uncovering further leads," Dorion informed the press.8

He also explained that police wanted Marguerite Pitre ("the crow") only for questioning. Police now believed Marie Ange Robitaille made up the third element in the love triangle. Dorion went on to say that Marguerite thought the parcel she'd been entrusted to deliver contained a statue, as she'd been told, not a weapon of mass murder.

Of course authorities hadn't been aware of her frantic phone call the day after the crash.

"My god, Al, what have we done?" the woman implored.

"It didn't go right, Marguerite," he answered. "The bomb should have gone off when the plane flew over the river, and the explosion should have started a fire. Whatever wasn't burned instantly should've been lost at the bottom of the St. Lawrence River. Something went wrong. The flight must have been delayed. Either that or my calculations were wrong by three or four minutes, five at the most."

Marguerite gasped. Could her frantic cab ride on September 9 somehow have contributed to the potentially damning miscue?

Albert continued, apparently unaware of Marguerite's reaction to his explanation, "Still, though, there's nothing to connect either one of us with the crash. Sure my wife was on board, but what does that prove? Lots of men's wives were on that plane."

"That's fine for you, Albert," the woman hissed angrily. "I'm the one who delivered the bomb to the airport."

"No one knows that particular delivery was the bomb. They just know there was a bomb on board," Albert suggested, attempting to placate his hyperventilating accomplice. "Look, Marguerite, if anyone should ask, tell them you thought you were delivering a box containing a statue. They can't prove that you knew what was in there."

A grunt on the other end of the phone line was Guay's only indication that Marguerite Pitre had heard his suggestion.

Calming considerably, Guay offered a consoling thought: "Besides, it won't come to that, Marguerite. This whole thing will blow over. A couple of weeks from now it'll be forgotten, as, of course, your debt to me already has been."

"All right, Albert, if you say so," the woman assented, desperately wanting to believe the man's statements. "But don't contact me. I don't want anyone to connect the two of us."

Deeply shaken by the possibility that her involvement in Canada's worst mass murder might be found out, the woman took a tranquilizer that her doctor had prescribed the previous week when she'd seen him for her "nerves."

Patience was not an abundant quality in Pitre at the best of times, and this was surely not "the best of times." To augment the effectiveness of the pill, she poured herself some generous ounces of cheap scotch. The woman desperately needed relief from the anxiety that had been her constant companion since that fateful trip to Ancienne Airport.

Guay carried the optimism he'd expressed to Marguerite when he saw her brother at the jewellery shop the next day.

"Don't worry, Genereux, my friend," he said trying to sound more confident than he felt. "There's nothing to connect either of us to the crash."

If any of the three murderers felt remorseful, they covered it well and only expressed concern that their part in a heinous crime might be detected.

Guay's facade of confidence did nothing to calm his own tightly strung nerves. He desperately wanted to believe the words he heard himself say to Genereux and Marguerite, but his instincts told him they were merely hollow invocations at best.

When the police arrived at Guay's place of business before store opening on Saturday, September 24, 1949, he greeted them with feelings of both relief and trepidation.

Clues implicating Guay in the murder of twenty-three innocent people piled one on top of another. While Guay had spent the days since the crash vacillating between feeling terror at the inevitability of being caught and experiencing an arrogant if false security that, at least so far, he'd gotten away with murder, the authorities assembled data. By the time they arrived at his jewellery shop, they had carefully compiled condemning evidence.

After allowing their suspect time to make arrangements to have his four-year old daughter taken care of, J. Albert Guay was led away in handcuffs, charged with the murder of his wife.

Genereux Ruest kept a low profile at the back of the store while the police were there. He assured his employer that it would be "business as usual" for that day anyway, and in turn Guay assured Ruest that he'd have this misunderstanding cleared up and would be back to open the store on Monday morning.

As the Quebec Provincial Police held the cruiser door open for an ashen-looking Guay, Genereux Ruest dialed his sister's phone number.

"Marguerite, they've got him. The police have arrested Albert and charged him with murder. My god, Marguerite, what do we do? In no time they'll know about us too." The man's mishapen body shook uncontrollably.

"Are you sure, Genereux? Are you sure it was about the bombing? You know Al's been arrested before. It might just be for some minor thing that we don't even know about." The woman knew she was grasping at straws but she also knew her life depended on the strength of her denial reflex.

"Yes, of course I'm sure. Listen to me. They've charged Albert with the murder of his wife."

A low moan escaped the woman's mouth as her obese body collapsed beside the dangling telephone receiver. Some moments later she struggled to her feet, placed the handset on the cradle of the phone and walked into the bathroom. The only solution to the dilemma rested on the medicine cabinet shelf. Rita Pitre, widow of Arthur Pitre, reached for a pill vial.

Her enormous bulk shook visibly and emitted primitive sounds, while she swallowed handful after handful of yellow tablets. She stumbled to her bed and, when the pills took the desired effect, Marguerite found herself, not at 49 Monseigneur Gauvreau Street in Lower Town Quebec City, but happily in a beautiful forest where ribbons of sunlight streaked through dark, leafy trees, and birds chirped musically. With a sigh, Marguerite Pitre's body sagged further into the peace she'd craved for so long.

Less than an hour later two police officers arrived at her door. Some of Guay's statements had made police interested in re-interviewing Marguerite. Another boarder in the Monseigneur Gauvreau Street house let them in and the constables knocked and called loudly at the entrance to the unconscious woman's flat. Despite their best efforts, Marguerite remained in her life-threatening, pharmacologically induced, idyllic forest setting. They tried the door, found it unlocked, and entered the suite, continuing to call loudly. The commotion alerted other residents to the unaccustomed excitement. Within minutes half a dozen boarders gathered around the door to the suite where Marguerite lay in the deadly arms of Morpheus. They talked excitedly among themselves, speculating about a myriad of possibilities.

Minutes later the screech of an ambulance siren increased the tension among the group. Falling silent, they cleared the way for three uniformed men carrying a stretcher into Pitre's rooms. The gap at the doorway closed behind the men and the chatter resumed. Shortly the scene replayed from the reverse angle. The three ambulance attendants assisted by the two police officers lugged the stretcher bearing the comatose Marguerite out of the house and into the waiting ambulance.

Even in those comparatively unenlightened days of medicine, doctors knew that the longer poison remained in the body the greater the potential damage. Minutes after her arrival at the Infant Jesus Hospital, medics unceremoniously emptied Marguerite's stomach of the self-administered toxins. A begrudging consciousness strained through to her drugged brain cells and, against her will, the woman's eyes fluttered open.

"Oh, mon dieu," the woman moaned, flailing against the restraints that held her to the gurney. "I want to be dead. Why am I not dead?"

"There, there, m'am," said a hospital matron who'd been sitting nearby. She had hurried to the suffering woman's side. "Please, please, let there be no such talk. It offends," she concluded, gesturing toward a small, inadequate-looking shelf supporting a bronze likeness of Mary holding the Christ child.

Marguerite closed her eyes in a vain attempt to return to her forest hideaway. It had gone. A not very subtle bump against her stretcher startled her eyes open once again.

"Madam Pitre, I am Inspector Rene Belec with the RCMP. I need to talk to you," the uniformed officer asserted.

Marguerite merely nodded, too weak and weary to protest.

"The information you give me will be passed on to the Quebec Provincial Police and the other investigators involved. You do not need to worry about having to endure many separate interviews," he explained, trying to entice Marguerite into giving complete and informative answers.

"I want to tell you everything. I must have this terrible thing off my mind or I will go mad," Marguerite asserted. "I fear it was I who delivered the bomb to that fatal flight."

After Willie Lamond's description of the woman who brought the parcel, this information was not really a revelation to the Inspector. Hearing it directly from her, however, strengthened the evidence.

"I swear to you I had no idea the package contained a bomb. He told me it was a gift for a friend in Baie Comeau — a statue. Had I known it was a bomb I'd never have agreed to do the favour."

"Of course, madam," the policeman consoled. "Who was it who asked you to do this favour?"

"Albert did," the woman admitted with fatigue in her voice. "Albert Guay, the jeweller. He gave me the parcel and asked me to take it to the airport in time to make the flight to Baie Comeau on September 9."

That was all Inspector Belec needed to hear. The "crow" had sung and now a direct connection between the bomb and Albert Guay existed.

"The hospital will be sending you home tomorrow. Some of my men will be going with you to keep watch over you. We don't want anymore of this," Belec explained, gesturing widely to include the hospital room where he stood beside Pitre's body overflowing the gurney. Glancing down at the woman, Rene Belec correctly assumed that she'd, once again, lost consciousness. Leaving a rookie constable to stand guard, the Inspector left the hospital with the damning information he needed to pursue the charge against Guay.

Although Belec felt no less appalled by the ghastly crime, the worst mass murder in Canadian history, he at least felt some small satisfaction that his efforts would be pivotal in bringing the reprehensible perpetrators to justice. He was also relieved — relieved that "the crow" had convinced him of her innocence. While reading the woman's twenty-six-page statement some days later, he felt pity for her. What a terrible thing Marguerite Pitre had been tricked into doing.

Many vocal citizens of Quebec City did not share Belec's surprisingly naive opinion. The next day police officers assigned to guard Marguerite Pitre against any further suicide attempts first needed to protect her from the wrath of an angry crowd gathered outside the rooming house she called home.

"Throughout the weekend crowds of men, women and children, who two days ago were startled to learn some of the rumors they had been hearing lately were true, stood outside the Pitre flat in a squalid section of Lower Town, hoping to catch a glimpse of the woman.

"But the window shades remained pulled down tight and the only sign of activity in front of the three-storey frame house was the coming and going of city constables stationed there.

"Although the throngs remained orderly last night, police said an angry mob had let loose a shower of cat-calls early yesterday morning. A stone was thrown through a front door, shattering the glass, and squads of uniformed constables were rushed to the scene when matters threatened to get out of hand."

"We have nothing against her," Belec offered to the press in the hope that those who made up the angry crowd would read it and be assuaged. "Mrs. Pitre was not a lover of Guay's but had simply been used as a tool ... to pull off the murder plot."9

He added that having officially laid the charge against Guay the police now concentrated their efforts on finding the person who built the bomb. They believed Guay hired someone to construct the intricate timing device. During the investigation into Guay's background, police discovered, among other things, that the man's abilities tended to be toward sales rather than the mechanical.

While twenty-three bodies lay cooling in their premature graves, and their families grieved and mourned, two court-appointed psychiatrists examined Albert Guay. They pronounced him "completely sane." 10

The court scheduled October 4, 1949, to begin the preliminary hearing, and Quebec Premier Maurice Duplessis, who also held the attorney general's portfolio, ordered a publication ban. Despite this dictate, the possible exhumation of Rita Guay's body and the connections among Marguerite Pitre, her highly skilled brother, Genereux Ruest, and the accused adorned the front page of the September 30, 1949, Montreal *Gazette*.11

Complete journalistic silence followed until the ides of March, 1950, when a lengthy headline summarized the story: "Near Record Set by Jury In Convicting Albert Guay, Guilty Verdict Given in 17 Minutes; Wife-murderer Sentenced to Be Hanged June 23; No Decision Yet on Appeal."12

Honouring the sanctity of the court, Judge Albert Sevigny wore long black robes and a tri-cornered hat. His voice choked with emotion as he pronounced the death sentence. The sixty-eight-year-old man had also occasionally wept openly during the thirteen-day trial.

During his summation to the jury, veteran Crown prosecutor Noel Dorion re-constructed the fatal sequence of events orchestrated by the condemned man. Guay purchased dynamite through an unnamed intermediary, arranged to have a sophisticated time-detonating mechanism and bomb manufactured and assembled, and had organized its delivery.

Before they retired, Sevigny advised the jury "they could not convict Guay on suspicion and because of the circumstantial nature of the evidence, [they] had to be certain the mass of ... testimony pointed straight at him."13

Seventeen minutes later, in reply to Judge Sevigny's official query, jury foreman and forestry engineer Paul Pouliot, replied in his native French, "coupable" (guilty).14

Although relieved by the jury's decision, Sevigny's anger and frustration at Guay's deranged, selfish and lethal act still raged.

> Albert Guay, the verdict which has been given against you means that the hatred you had for your wife, and the vice that gnawed at you, made you commit the diabolical crime of which you have been accused.
>
> The vicious passion, which drove you to the conquest of a young girl disgusted with you, led you to this incredible thing of not hesitating to bring death to twenty-two other persons to rid yourself of the mother of your child.
>
> Your punishment will be to be hanged by the neck, June 23, next, until death. J. Albert Guay, have you anything to say?[15]

Guay's face revealed little of what he might have been feeling or thinking while listening to the verdict and the judge's words. In a barely audible voice he replied, "Non."

"Pale and shaky on his feet ... Guay then followed two police officers through a door behind the prisoner's box and out of sight." [16]

He did not hear the judge compliment the jury on a "good verdict and their conduct during the ... trial."[17]

The date established for Guay's execution was doubly ironic: not only was it the eve of the feast of St. Jean-Baptiste Day, Quebec's annual day of celebrations, but also the anniversary of the incident that instigated the horrible sequence of events. It had been on June 23, 1949, that a frightened Marie-Ange Robitaille called the police to report that Albert Guay was waving a revolver about and uttering threats to her life and well-being.

Initially, Guay seemed determined to spend his last weeks on this earth in despondent introspection. He made no attempt to appeal the jury's verdict. It took Crown prosecutor Dorion by surprise when, a month later, Guay summoned the lawyer to visit him in his death cell. The condemned man had a statement to make — a one-hundred-and-fourteen-page statement.

Albert Guay wanted the world to know that both Marguerite Pitre and Genereux Ruest knew from the beginning that they would be playing pivotal roles in Canada's most horrendous mass murder. Further, that they had agreed to accept their part in order to gain financial compensation.

Police arrested Ruest and Pitre. Guay's execution was postponed so he could testify at their trials. He did not gain many additional months of life but they were no doubt satisfying to his demented mind, for on December 14, 1950, Guay witnessed fifty-four year old Ruest, described as a "little ... crutch-carrying cripple," being sentenced to death. Showing astounding insensitivity, the Montreal *Gazette* described "the ... watchmaker hobbling off in the footsteps of ... J. Albert Guay." [18]

Guay also lived long enough to know that his former friend and work-mate, Marguerite Pitre, would soon be joining her brother and himself in the hereafter.

On Friday, January 12, 1951, at 12:40 a.m. Guay walked to the scaffold accompanied by Reverence Lucien Cleremont, the chaplain of Montreal's Bordeaux Jail. Acting Deputy Chief A. Guillemmette, Captain J.A. Matte and Lieutenant Martin Healey, all of the QPP and Constables J.E. Belanger and A.H. Scott of the CPR police were present as witnesses to the hanging.

Knowing no hope remained, Guay told guards, "At least I'll die famous."[19] He waited patiently while the hangman adjusted the noose. Once the rope was judged to be effectively placed, Guay offered to shake hands with his guards, the chaplain and the sheriff, Paul Hurteau. If they accepted his offer the fact wasn't recorded.

This DC-3 is a sister plane of the one bombed by Albert Guay, with the help of Marguerite Pitre and her brother Genereux Ruest in 1949.

The DC-3 (Douglas Commercial, third generation) first flew in December, 1935. It was acknowledged as one of the greatest airliners ever built. The plane was structurally so sound that it outlasted many models which were designed to replace it. With the outbreak of World War II, the DC-3 (also known as the Dakota, the Sky Train, the Sky Trooper and the Gooney Bird) went from strictly commercial use to troop carrier, supply plane and glider tug. After the war, many were re-fitted for commercial use; others served in both the Korean and the Vietnam wars. To date, some DC-3s remain in service. (Photo courtesy of Canadian Airlines.)

At 12:43 a.m. the trap door beneath the prisoner's feet released. The rope extended to its fatal, taut end, tightening the noose and snapping the convicted man's neck. Exactly five minutes later, at 12:48 a.m., Dr. Romeo Plouffe pronounced Guay dead.

* * *

Despite appeals that carried his case all the way to the Supreme Court of Canada, Genereux Ruest was wheeled to the same gallows on July 25, 1952.

During the unsuccessful attempts to stay her brother's death, a jury of her peers convicted Marguerite Pitre of being a party to the dreadful airborne fatalities of September 9, 1949. This charge added to the two she'd collected during her brother's trial — "intimidation of a witness" and "giving perjured evidence." The judge, Mr. Justice Fernand Choquette, ruled that Marguerite be held without bail.

As her brother had done, the woman launched a series of futile appeals. But on January 9, 1953, the trap door at Montreal's Bordeaux Jail opened once again to drop Marguerite Pitre to her place in history — the last woman executed in Canada.

WHEN TORONTO-THE-GOOD WENT BAD

In 1949, the horrors that World War II had brought to people's lives finally began to feel more like recent history than current events. The Great Depression, now relegated to a niche in the memory banks of those who had suffered through it, became a topic only when trying to impress upon the day's wretched and ungrateful youth just what fortunate times they lived in.

With steadily rising employment, the collective philosophy held that anyone willing to work hard and live sensibly would prosper. In short, life held nothing but promise and hope.

On the morning of September 9, 1949, Edwin Alonzo Boyd, son of a retired Toronto police officer, was a hopeful man, too, but he also had some concerns. He'd never robbed a bank before.

When Bank of Montreal manager George Elwood opened the doors of his Armour Heights branch, he radiated hope: he looked forward to a busier than normal Friday. Toronto's annual institution, The Canadian National Exhibition, would close the next evening and the experienced bank manager predicted many of his clients would want extra cash to enjoy one last frolic at the "Ex."

Elwood and his staff knew and liked most of their clients. Businesses up and down Avenue Road made up a large percentage of the branch's commercial business. Many owners of the comfortable brick homes that lined the streets to the east and west of the mercantile strip held savings and chequing accounts at his branch. Elwood felt proud of the position he had earned both at the bank and in the community.

Boyd, on the other hand, had been feeling unsatisfied with the meager existence he'd been able to eke out for himself and his growing family since the end of the war. Eddie had served in the army's Provost Corps both before and during the war — an ironic posting, because he'd done time for a number of petty thefts. These offenses had all been committed during the Depression and, unofficially at least, most people viewed the theft of food and money during those times as an economic necessity.

Boyd thrived on the excitement of the war years. Like many young men who'd spent the Dirty Thirties riding the rails, moving from one hobo camp to another in a vain attempt to find employment, enlisting brought more than just financial relief. It brought travel *and* adventure. And the Canadian government saw fit to widen Eddie's territory considerably. They sent him overseas.

Ed's rugged good looks always made him popular with women. With potential admirers in both continental Europe and Britain how could he go wrong? He couldn't and he didn't. Not long after his arrival in England, Boyd requested permission to marry. A young school teacher had stolen Ed's heart. Nothing would do but she had to become Mrs. Edwin Alonzo Boyd. Nothing, that is, except the return of her boyfriend.

Never one to let adversity get him down, Ed accepted the woman's change of heart like a gentleman. Within days, he met and proposed to the beautiful young Doreen Mary Frances Thompson. Merely substituting her name on the marriage application, the two formed a union that lasted through some incredible adversities.

Shortly after the war ended, the Boyds moved from England to Eddie's hometown, Toronto, where he found work as a driver for the Toronto Transit Commission. Driving a streetcar, however, didn't come close to providing the adrenaline rushes he sought, and that work lasted less than a year.

A number of dead-end jobs followed, none of any great length or significance. Eddie became discouraged and distraught. He complained that the country he'd served, at great risk, was now not willing to give him a break.

It's hard to be sympathetic to the man's pleas. He'd found steady employment, adequate housing, a wife and now three children whom he adored — not bad for a young man assessed as only an "adequate" pupil in school and with a criminal record to boot.

But Boyd dreamed of greater things — fame and wealth. At thirty-five his lust for action and adventure took over and earned him a significant place in the criminal history of Canada.

From a perspective of nearly fifty years it is difficult to separate legend from reality. The most accepted version of the story goes something like this: Boyd heard or read about a mentally retarded teenager successfully robbing a bank of nearly $70,000. Police caught the boy shortly after the heist but that didn't deter Boyd. He was nothing if not self confident. Some might even have called him arrogant. There was no question in Boyd's mind that he could improve on the work of a handicapped child.

At that time, three newspapers competed on a daily basis for Torontonians attention. The two evening papers, the *Daily Star* and the *Telegram,* in direct competition, fought long and hard to win, not only their readers' eighteen cents a week, but their loyalty. An objective analysis of the hard news indicates this rivalry went a long way toward creating the legend that has become "The Boyd Gang."

The bare facts fall considerably short of substantiating the legend. In an introduction to their book, *The Boyd Gang*, Barry Pearson and Marjorie Lamb state, "The gang's exploits made such good copy that news writers were encouraged to embroider and extend the known facts with their own inventions."[1] Readers lapped it up. As devastating as it had been, the war had provided an aspect of excitement to people's everyday lives. Now, accounts of a gang of criminals, in Toronto-the-Good, brought that excitement back — back in a safer and less obtrusive way than the war. In this context the Boyd Gang and the popular conception of Edwin Alonzo Boyd, the folk hero, was born.

Eddie prepared carefully for his first "job." He'd been into the Armour Heights branch of the Bank of Montreal on several occasions. He used ploys such as inquiries about services available or hours of business and needing change as ruses to justify having a good look around. On the morning of September 9, he only needed to make final personal preparations.

Boyd disguised himself by stuffing cotton batting into his mouth, to distend and distort the lower part of his face. This altered his appearance dramatically but did nothing to calm his nerves. A shot of Irish whisky fulfilled that function, and with his army revolver stuffed in the waistband of his trousers, he set off to start his career change.

For a man with no experience in the field, Eddie did all right in his first "job." He withdrew $2,300 from a bank where he had no account and escaped successfully, on foot. As a fringe benefit, the episode provided him with some very valuable, job-related lessons: he never again chose to fortify his courage with alcohol, and the importance of clearly defined getaway arrangements had become dramatically obvious. Still, though, for just a few seconds of foolhardy bravery and, of course, a willingness to forget the moral teachings of his youth, Boyd profited roughly a year's wages.

Predictably, the money ran out far more quickly than regularly scheduled wage payments might have. And so, early in the new year Boyd began preparations for his second heist. He'd carefully read all the newspaper reports on his last holdup, and he felt well prepared for the job at hand when, on January 18, 1950, he pulled up outside an east-end branch of the Canadian Bank of Commerce. He left a stolen 1949 Ford idling at the curb while he did his banking. This time the haul was even better, just under $3,000. Again, though, the getaway was rough. The bank's accountant, angered by the intrusion, pursued Boyd and came very close to catching him. Perhaps Eddie needed a partner. That thought planted a seed for the beginnings of the Boyd Gang.

Pearson and Lamb explain: "The perfect partner would be a man who was easily led, needed money, had experience robbing banks, but was not necessarily too smart. With luck he would be fast on his feet and at ease with a weapon. Those were the ideal qualifications, but Boyd could hardly take out a classified ad to find his accomplice."[2]

And so Boyd began looking for a business partner in less conventional ways. He happened upon an ex-prison guard Howard Gault, who actually held very few of the qualifications Boyd originally had in mind. But through his training at Burwash Reformatory, Gault knew guns and, most importantly, he needed money badly enough to take the risks involved in joining Boyd's escapades.

By closing time on July 31, 1950, a Dominion Bank in northwest Toronto was short just under $2,000 and a .38 revolver.

These robberies not only frustrated the police but they angered Mayor Allan Lamport. Never one to back away from either controversy or the spotlight, Lamport lashed out at what he saw as invitingly lax security measures in Toronto's banks. He insisted they be better prepared to protect themselves against armed robbers.

"We can never have enough policemen if easy money in banks lies around. Men read in the newspapers how thousands were stolen from a bank and how the getaway was fairly easy, and they see a way to get enough money to last them for a couple of years."[3]

Lamport's outburst may have contributed substantially to the speedy arrest and conviction of a man named Peter Marino for the end-of-July holdup committed by Gault and Boyd. That erroneous conviction bought Boyd some time to think. He decided that he worked better alone. Gault's presence during the robbery accomplished little except to cut Boyd's income by half. Being considerably older, Gault lacked the physical prowess and agility that Boyd prided himself on. By this, his third profitable bank robbery, Eddie had developed a recognizable style that included vaulting over counters.

Again Boyd pondered his future. He wasn't qualified for any other job that paid nearly as well as robbing banks did. The benefits of taking a partner into his fledgling business had not turned out well. He vowed to return to single proprietorship.

On October 11, 1950, a glorious autumn day in Toronto, Ed Boyd did just that. This time he targeted an Imperial Bank of Canada on Avenue Road, a few blocks south of his first-ever robbery just over a year before. During those intervening thirteen months and three successful thefts, Boyd learned many useful new job-related skills. Unfortunately for him, bank employees developed as sincere an interest in keeping their customers' money as Boyd had in relieving them of it.

Boyd's very success now began to work against him. The element of surprise, once a powerful weapon for his whirlwind banking expeditions, no longer existed. His daring exploits dramatically raised the awareness of every bank employee in the Toronto area. And so, the sudden commotion in front of his office provided manager W.H.G. Smith with all the warning he needed. He reached for his loaded gun and came out of his office ready to do battle.

Boyd and Smith each maintained the other took the first shot. The flying bullets, however, missed their targets and lodged harmlessly in the bank's walls. Despite his love of excitement and easy money, Boyd was not, by nature, a cruel man, and it surprised and offended him when he realized the bank's employees might try to hurt him.

Part of the Boyd legend holds that for over a year Doreen Boyd remained unaware of her husband's exploits. This supposed naivety undoubtedly increased the woman's later public appeal considerably. The romantic scenario, however, seems distinctly unlikely. One facet of Mr. and Mrs. Boyd's relationship is beyond doubt — the intense passion they felt for one another. Eddie adored Doreen and their children, and they him.

Badly frightened by what he viewed as his brush with death, Boyd once again applied to the City of Toronto for employment. The Works Department needed labourers, and early in November 1950 Boyd joined his former accomplice, Howard Gault, on a road repair crew. It didn't pay nearly as well as their previous partnership and was deathly boring.

Evidently the combination of boredom and small pay cheques got the best of Eddie's intentions, and so on March 19, 1951, he once again held up the Bank of Montreal, Armour Heights branch.

Newspapers reported the take as $6,000. Boyd's version indicates he made off with about half that amount.[4] Oddly, the next day he returned to his $1.10-an-hour job behind an asphalt burner on the city streets. He remained gainfully employed until July 31, 1951, when a truck passing the work crew struck Boyd, injuring his shoulder slightly.

The accident marked the end of any attempt to earn an honest living. Years afterward, trying to shift responsibility for his crimes away from himself, Boyd remembered the incident. He maintained the Compensation Board unfairly denied his application for benefits and that their decision left him without recourse but to return to robbing banks in order to support his family.

Fortunately he'd had the foresight to tuck away much of the profit from his second trip to the teller's cage at the Bank of Montreal. Through the Department of Veterans' Affairs, Boyd bought a residential lot in the town of Pickering, just northeast of Toronto, and there he and Doreen spent the summer of 1951 contently building a small home.

As Mayor Lamport predicted, others with an interest in easy money noted Boyd's success as a bank robber. While Boyd toiled away in Pickering, other thieves kept the banks and police forces in southern Ontario wondering who, what or where the next target would be. The news that a group of thugs had recently executed its fourth profitable armed robbery in a matter of weeks diverted Boyd's attention from construction.

Team work apparently had advantages. Boyd called his youngest brother, Norman, and his old friend Howard Gault. On Saturday, September 1, 1951, he parked his truck near the Jolly Miller Hotel on Yonge Street at the north end of Toronto. The Boyd brothers, accompanied by Howard Gault, then stole a car, drove north to Willowdale's Sheppard Avenue and east to the Lansing Branch of Dominion Bank. For disguise, they smudged their faces with dirt and wore dirty clothes. Minutes later, they left the bank $8,000 richer and Eddie Boyd knew he could never return to salaried employment again.

Some months later police arrested Norman, Ed's brother, and charged him with being part of that holdup. The younger man's subsequent release on a technicality served to reinforce Eddie Boyd's delusions of being above the law.

Police in the Toronto area knew they had to stop this rash of bank robberies. Chief John Chisholm put Sergeant Dolph Payne in charge of bringing the criminals to justice. While the sergeant carefully and quietly investigated and re-investigated each detail of the recent holdups, Eddie and Gault boldly designed their next one.

On October 16, 1951, the two men left Boyd's truck in the parking lot of the Fairlawn movie theatre on Yonge Street, north of Lawrence Avenue. This time, to disguise themselves, they both removed their false teeth and left them in the truck. Now, toothless but confident, the pair stole a nearby sedan and drove a few blocks south to the Dominion Bank.

Having such a string of successes to his credit, Eddie felt in complete control and with gun drawn, he ordered the employees to a corner of the bank. However, one employee escaped his vigilance. Adelene Jamieson inched her way toward the bank's alarm. The pair's luck had run out.

Boyd's agility and fitness gave him the advantage of a clean getaway. Gault's nervousness and age proved his downfall. Weighted down with the bag of loot, the older man tripped as he left the bank. Just as he recovered his balance and a grip on the money, constables Walter McLean and Frank Skelly arrived at the scene of the crime. Gault managed to elude the police briefly, and make his way on foot a few blocks down the street.

Boyd sped away in the waiting stolen car, a steady stream of bullets from constable McLean's service revolver cascading around him.

Gault's flight drew the attention of a passing motorcycle cop. This officer left his motorcycle to join the foot chase and he quickly gained on the tooth-less Gault. Realizing the officer would soon be within firing range, the exhausted bandit threw down the bag of money and gave himself up. Half an hour later, other officers pulled Boyd over in his truck. Their drawn guns convinced him he'd finally lost a round.

While the arresting officers processed paperwork necessary for the two arrests, a detective named Lorimer emptied Boyd's truck of what were undeniably burglary tools and a set of dentures. Considerately, the officer returned Gault's false teeth. The fate of Boyd's teeth isn't known.

The gun the older man had used during the holdup belonged to the Dominion Bank that he and Boyd had robbed the previous summer. Undoubtedly it pleased that bank's staff to have the gun returned, but no one was as happy as Peter Marino who'd been serving time for the robbery while steadfastly maintaining his innocence. Officials released him immediately.

Guards marched Edwin Alonzo Boyd through the corridors of the gothic Don Jail with an air of accomplishment and closure. At last, good triumphed over at least two who had consistently and profitably offended Toronto's well-ingrained protestant work ethic. With Boyd's arrest, the worst string of bank robberies in the city's history ended.

Did Boyd feel a sense of defeat as the iron bars of his cell door swung shut behind him? If he did, he made sure he didn't reveal his emotions. He wouldn't allow those who'd captured him the satisfaction of thinking they'd also arrested and imprisoned his spirit. Besides, as luck would have it, that cold, ugly, iron-and-stone holding cell served as the birthing room for the Boyd Gang.

As the guard's footsteps receded along the cement corridor, Eddie heard a voice from the next cell: "Welcome, we've been expecting you."

A combination of overcrowding and a complete lack of thought landed the newly arrested robber next door to another veteran of the trade.

"I'm Lennie Jackson," the voice continued. "Me and my friends admire your work. We've pulled off a few in our time, too. You might have heard of us. We managed all those heists this past summer."

A small smile spread across Boyd's face. Here he stood, near the man who'd made headlines during the months the Boyds built their house in Pickering. Life's little ironies continued to delight.

Jackson didn't think much of the life provided for him in jail. He'd made an escape attempt just days before Boyd's arrival. Now fate saw fit to hand him another five-star thief as a neighbour. No sensible person could expect this amount of criminal talent to remain behind bars for long. And it didn't.

With another prisoner, William R. Jackson (no relation to Lennie), the three escaped from the Don Jail unnoticed. In broad daylight, on the unseasonably cold afternoon of Sunday, November 4, they shimmied down a rope of bed sheets they'd borrowed from their fellow prisoners and away to freedom.

Like Boyd, Leonard Jackson had spent time riding the rails. The standard procedure for non-paying passengers required that they board trains considerably after the traditional bellow of "all aboard." This routine required strength and split-second timing; even a slight slip could be fatal. Leonard Jackson knew the dangers from personal experience. In 1948, as he attempted to climb aboard a train leaving the Toronto rail yards, he misjudged the distance and the train's speed. The error cost Lennie his left foot.

This disability was one of the reasons he'd made arrangements to have his old friend and accomplice Steve Suchan pick them up near the jail. During his youth Suchan showed tremendous promise as a musician. The teenager had conscientiously studied his beloved violin while his peers enjoyed less esoteric activities. For unrecorded reasons Steve, in his early twenties, suddenly abandoned this admirable dedication to music and turned his energies, instead, to a life of crime.

Unfortunately for the escapees, Suchan's obligation to his friends that Sunday had slipped his mind completely. While Boyd and the two Jackson's may have been angry, they could certainly understand how the presence of a beautiful woman, such as Suchan's girlfriend, Lennie's sister, could cause temporary amnesia.

While Lennie phoned the distracted Steve Suchan and then his own girlfriend, Ann Roberts, Boyd fumed. Willie Jackson, always the clown, tried to humour Eddie.

Willie had been born in "Cabbagetown," the slums of Toronto, to parents deemed by the Children's Aid Society to be "unfit." He first saw the inside of a penal institution before his sixteenth birthday. His life so far had been a series of illegal escapades, arrests and escapes. This current situation which had so upset his partners was highly entertaining to Willie "the clown."

As these three disparate personalities waited to be picked up by a fourth, the guards at the Don Jail were also making phone calls — a turnkey had noted the escape not long after dinner. Officials contacted police departments for miles around as well as personnel at border-crossing points. The convicts would not get far if the forces of justice could help it.

Boyd and his cronies may have suspected they'd be caught if they tried to escape from the area, or they may not have seen much advantage in such effort. Lennie Jackson and his girlfriend, Ann, did make their way to a motel near Oshawa, but Boyd and Willie Jackson accepted hospitality much closer to home. They stayed at a boarding house run by Steve Suchan's parents.

Although Boyd enjoyed the comfortable hideaway and the generous home-cooked meals, he knew he needed money. Doreen and the children

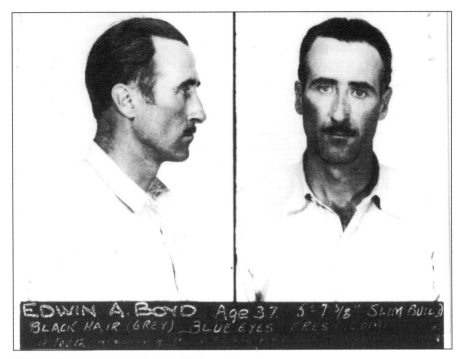

Toronto police's mug shots of Edwin Boyd. (Courtesy of the Toronto Police Museum.)

were safe enough in the still-incomplete house on Rosemount Drive in Pickering, but they had no income. Mortgages, groceries and utility bills needed payment. Boyd could hardly re-apply to the city for employment at this point and so he planned his first "job" as leader of the Boyd Gang.

On November 20, 1951, just over two weeks after they'd broken out of the Don Jail, Boyd, the two Jacksons, Steve Suchan and possibly Norman Boyd entered a west-end branch of the Bank of Toronto which had been open for business less than half an hour. The gang's organization and speed left the startled employees unable to agree on the number of robbers or what any of them looked like.

About the only consistent statement indicated that the group had been led by a "toothless master mind."[5] From this police deduced, correctly, that the robbery had been the work of Eddie Boyd and, probably, his fellow escapees.

For all the expertise the fledgling gang represented, their take only totalled $4,300, far short of the amount needed to meet all of their needs. They would have to choose their "target markets" more carefully.

Toronto police's mug shots of Leonard Jackson. (Courtesy of the Toronto Police Museum.)

And so they did. They selected a branch of the Royal Bank in Toronto's Leaside community. Boyd suspected that many workers from nearby factories cashed their paycheques there, and so on Fridays the bank would keep extra money on hand.

Boyd's presumptions proved correct. On Friday, November 30, bank manager Albert Hockley arranged to have approximately $100,000 on hand; before noon the Boyd Gang had reduced that sum by almost half.

The holdup bore many of the qualities that made a Boyd job recognizable. Heavily armed, the robbers appeared extremely self-assured. Before they fled they calmly commented to one another that they thought they had enough money. As usual they'd stolen a car to use as a getaway vehicle. As an extra precaution they'd changed the car's licence plates to those stolen from a second car. During their getaway, they abandoned that vehicle and either picked up one of their own or walked to Suchan's parents' rooming house where they could divide the take.

Boyd thought they should give Suchan's parents a percentage of the take. After all, they'd been providing Boyd, Suchan, and William Jackson with protection since their breakout. Suchan assured Boyd he'd take care of it. Much to

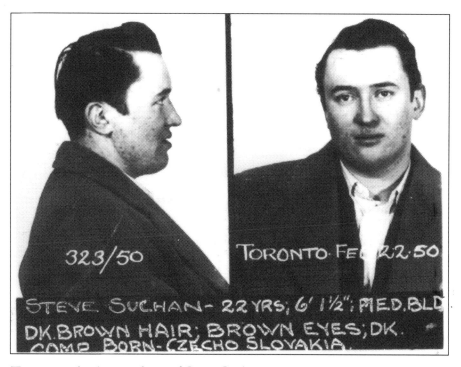

Toronto police's mug shots of Steve Suchan. (Courtesy of the Toronto Police Museum.)

Boyd's anger and frustration, Suchan's idea of "taking care of it" wasn't the same as his. This misunderstanding resulted in a large part of the stolen money being re-stolen — by the elder Suchan who, shortly after, sent his wife and the group of boarders a postcard from Florida.

The future did not look assured for Eddie Boyd. Police wanted him for breaking out of jail and now two additional bank robberies, but neither he nor his wife and three children were much better off financially than they had been.

About this time the press began referring to "the Boyd Gang" as though it were an established entity. So far, Boyd's accomplices had varied from job to job and this pattern continued. The assorted confederates' actions during their last months of freedom didn't reflect any sort of cohesive thinking.

It's likely that the press merely echoed the terminology used by American reporters some years before. During the 1920s, gangs dominated many U.S. cities. The resulting terror bore more than a passing resemblance to the then present situation in "Toronto-the-Good."

The debate as to whether an actual "gang" ever existed could go on endlessly, but, at this point, the robbers began to go their separate ways.

Steve Suchan's and Lennie Jackson's funds remained intact. Boyd's and Willie Jackson's money was soaking up sun with Suchan's father. Boyd suggested that the four pool the funds on hand and re-divide what remained. Neither Steve nor Lennie agreed and both, wisely, decided to stay out of Boyd's way for awhile.

Lennie took his girlfriend, Ann Roberts, to live in Montreal. Steve Suchan and Mary Mitchell, Lennie's sister (and the reason Suchan had been late picking up the escaped convicts earlier in the month), followed. A few weeks later, Eddie and Doreen Boyd, and Willie Jackson, also headed for the more cosmopolitan city.

Willie's freedom didn't last long. A week before Christmas, he excused himself from the lady-friend with whom he'd been sharing a social drink in a lounge and went to the men's room. While there, his suit coat came open revealing the gun he always carried. The glint of metal upset the patron at the next urinal sufficiently that he called the police. Just minutes later, William R. Jackson was back in custody.

The Toronto police were not only pleased to have Jackson under lock and key but to learn why their Toronto-based searches were coming up dry. Willie had two additional years added to his sentence and travelled, at government expense, to Kingston. Toronto police alerted their Montreal counterparts to be on the lookout for the rest of the gang. But just at that same time, Eddie Boyd, Steve Suchan, Lennie Jackson and their female companions wisely decided to leave the area and spend Christmas in Toronto.

The Boyds couldn't very well go to their home in Pickering so they settled for a room in a motel on Toronto's Lake Shore Boulevard. Mary Mitchell and Steve Suchan were their next-door neighbours and the four, along with the three Boyd children, spent an uneventful and reportedly pleasant Christmas together.

A most intriguing device in the lobby of their motel-cum-temporary-home kept Boyd's children fascinated for hours on end. Here they watched slightly fuzzy, black-and-white images dart across a round screen. What a novelty! Doreen Boyd was one of the first mothers to discover television's qualities as an effective babysitter.

A few days after Christmas the Boyds decided to move back to their home in Pickering. As Doreen was once quoted as saying, "You can't say he hasn't got guts. Maybe he doesn't use them the right way, but he certainly has them."[6]

Lennie Jackson married Ann Roberts on January 2, 1952. They immediately headed off on their honeymoon — a car trip to western Canada, which kept them safely out of either Toronto or Montreal until the first week of February.

About this time Steve Suchan proved that his personal moral standards were no higher than his business ones. He maintained a very close relationship with Mary Mitchell but on January 12, a woman named Anna Bosnich gave birth to his son.

Only William Jackson's life remained unchanged. He continued to reside in the Kingston Penitentiary. Willie's brother, Joseph, however, did not, and that's who Eddie Boyd contacted when he needed an accomplice for a hold-up he planned for January 25, 1952. He also enlisted Steve Suchan.

By the end of that business day, the Bank of Toronto on Kingston Road was short some $10,000 and a revolver. Bank staff and police identified the maneuver as a Boyd Gang job. Three well-dressed men entered the branch, vaulted the counters and took immediate control. They were the picture of confidence. A teller reported that one bandit even smiled at her during the robbery. Again, a stolen car bearing stolen plates served as an effective getaway vehicle.

All three were eventually charged with the crime but, amazingly, none were convicted.

Frustration ate at Toronto's police force. Allan Lamport, as mayor, was his usual vocal self. Sergeant of Detectives Edmund Tong and Sergeant Dolph Payne devoted themselves almost entirely to apprehending the various members of the notorious Boyd Gang.

Steve Suchan happily deluded himself into thinking his arrangement of living with Mary Mitchell and fathering Anna Bosnich's child suited everyone involved. It didn't. He had, predictably, become smitten with his infant son, which gave Anna a position of power in the triangle. The arrangement did not please Mitchell, and she was not about to suffer in silence. She'd been active in the gang for a number of months, having driven getaway cars, made motel arrangements, and even posed as an informer with Sergeant of Detectives Tong. Mary Mitchell thrived on all the drama and excitement of her associations. This was not a woman who would have settled for a librarian's life.

Tong's interest in Mitchell as an informant wasn't surprising. As Leonard Jackson's half-sister and the full sister to Kingston Penitentiary convict Sam Stone, Mitchell was a potentially valuable resource for the police.

Eddie Boyd had become suspicious of the woman's allegiances on a number of occasions, and he would have been wise to trust his instincts. Perhaps he didn't fully appreciate how deeply Suchan's betrayal angered and hurt Mitchell.

Immediately after visiting Tong, Mary Mitchell arranged to see Steve Suchan. She displayed an ugly collection of what appeared to be cigarette burns on her chest, claiming to Suchan that Tong tortured her into giving him information. In desperation, Mitchell claimed, she'd told Tong that

Suchan spent a lot of time at Anna Bosnich's home and had given a detailed description of her car, which Suchan frequently drove.

"So, Steve, you'd better stay away from Anna's place for awhile. They'll be watching for you there," she concluded smugly.

The version of the story told by the Toronto Police differs only in that no one there tortured Mary Mitchell, that she willingly and eagerly gave Tong the information about Suchan's whereabouts, and that the burns were likely self-inflicted.

Suchan's double love life and the resulting contradictory allegiances proved to be fatally pivotal details for the Boyd Gang.

Eddie, however, continued to further his career as bank-robber-extraordinaire. With many of his usual partners otherwise engaged, Boyd, Willie "the clown" Jackson and Allister Gibson, Willie's brother-in-law, relieved the Bank of Montreal, College and Manning branch, of $24,696.

Two days later, on March 6, 1952, police officers Perry and Tong were patrolling near Anna Bosnich's home. Early in the afternoon they spotted her black Monarch car. The officers pursued it until both vehicles reached a red light where they ordered the two male occupants to pull over. Tong, naively, got out of the cruiser and approached the escaped convicts. Steve Suchan fired his pistol through the driver's side window, hitting Tong in his chest, slightly to the left of centre. As Tong fell to the road, Suchan continued to fire toward the cruiser.

Leonard Jackson leapt from the car, firing wildly. A bullet from Jackson's rifle grazed Sergeant Perry's arm as the officer lifted it to protect his head from the onslaught of bullets.

Jackson and Suchan realized they'd hit both officers. The traffic light in front of them had turned red again, but the Monarch gunned through the intersection leaving Tong dying on the street and Perry struggling to radio for help.

The escaping pair drove the highly recognizable car to a residential street and then abandoned it in favour of a much more anonymous taxi cab.

When help arrived for the injured police officers, witnesses noted that Tong's gun remained in its holster. As his fellow officers rushed to comfort their colleagues, Tong struggled to tell them he'd recognized Steve Suchan as the gunman. Emergency workers loaded the injured men into an ambulance which then sped toward the Toronto General Hospital.

Suchan phoned Anna and told her to contact the police and report her car stolen. He refused to explain his demand. Moments after she'd made the call, the boys in blue arrived at her door, but Anna's "stolen" car was not at the top of their agenda.

Police and media immediately broadcast descriptions of Leonard Jackson and Steve Suchan. Interestingly, they estimated Suchan's age at between thirty-five and thirty-eight. In fact Steve was a mere twenty-four. Urgent pleas were issued to Toronto citizens to donate blood for the critically injured Tong.

The Toronto *Telegram* proclaimed: "Gunmen Hunted by 1,000 Officers."[7] Eddie Boyd, who was returning from an evening at the movies with Doreen, saw the headline and not far under it, his own name, so they purchased a supply of groceries and went into hiding.

Suchan and Jackson made their way, by cab, to Hamilton, sixty kilometres southwest of Toronto, but once there they realized they'd be safer in Montreal where Jackson's wife waited for him, and Suchan had a disguised identity and an apartment. They stole a car and drove through the night while Tong fought for his life, and his colleagues searched for the gunmen.

When they reached Montreal the pair split up. Suchan saw cash as his immediate need and set about selling his 1951 Chrysler. While he was away from his apartment, Montreal police arrived and talked the building manager into opening Suchan's suite for them. When the young desperado returned home he'd taken only half a dozen steps into the apartment before three bullets hit his torso in rapid succession. Now Suchan, like his victim Edwin Tong, lay in a hospital bed fighting for his life. Tong, however, wasn't manacled to the bed.

Only two blocks away, Leonard and Ann Jackson hid in their apartment, and when they heard about Suchan's arrest over the radio, they probably realized their own arrests were imminent. Their photographs appeared on the front pages of both Montreal and Toronto newspapers. Inevitably, neighbours recognized the couple they knew as "Mr. and Mrs. Wilson" and advised the police. The $12,500 reward might well have contributed to their sense of justice.

Whatever the informants' motivation, the police were grateful for the tip. Early on the evening of March 11, 1952, heavily armed Montreal police, accompanied by a contingent from Toronto, arrived at the "Wilson's" door. A wild gun battle ensued. One of the first bullets fired hit and injured Jackson but he continued shooting at the half dozen officers.

The bullet wound must have caused Jackson to forget his manners: he grabbed his wife and held her in front of him as a shield. His presumption that the police wouldn't want to injure Ann proved to be correct; however, when she screamed and struggled, Jackson pushed her to the floor.

Outside, police reinforcements sped toward the stand-off, bringing a supply of tear gas. Shortly after, the pair staggered into the waiting handcuffs of the officers.

Despite having been shot and gassed, Jackson managed to remain aggressive as police led him away. He told the crowd which had been attracted by the gun battle that he knew who "ratted" on him and would make sure Boyd came after those responsible.

This sensational, but empty, claim very effectively perpetuated the Boyd Gang myth, which, to a large degree, had been generated by the media's more dramatic than accurate reporting style. Those watching the spectacular arrest could not have known that Leonard Jackson hadn't had contact with Eddie Boyd since November 30, 1951, when they'd robbed the Royal Bank in Leaside together.

Inspired by their success and a series of fictitious tips, police began to comb the city for Boyd. A lieutenant with the provincial police described the unfocused searching techniques this way, "You raid here, you raid there. Sometimes you score, sometimes you don't."[8]

Toronto's *Telegram* described the situation in a series of three photographs and a single word headline, "HUNTED."[9] Under the bold-faced word, were pictures of Boyd flanked by Leonard Jackson and Steve Suchan. Large black "X"s covered the faces of the two apprehended men and only Boyd's face looked out at the readers. Police, media and Canadians in general wanted an end to this lawlessness, and the headline indicated the arrests were taking place in an expected sequence. This hopefulness was probaly intended to shore up morale and reputations.

Edwin and Doreen Boyd had placed their three children in a boarding school and, with Norman, rented an apartment on the second floor of a house in a residential section of Toronto. They told the landlord they were visiting missionaries.

Although they were unaware of it, they were under constant police surveillance. Authorities prepared for this arrest with the greatest care and attention. The owner of the house next door to the "missionaries" apartment allowed officers to use their livingroom as a stakeout. The police said they were on the track of some bootleggers. In that era, no self-respecting citizen of Toronto-the-Good would stand in the way of the police protecting the unsuspecting citizenry from the evils of intemperance.

Throughout the night of March 14 and into the early morning hours of March 15, police surrounded the house where the three Boyds slept peacefully in mistaken security. In organizing this raid, police authorities repeatedly reviewed the plan until they knew they had it right. They could not take a chance on Boyd escaping; they might never be able to track him down and corner him so effectively again. They accounted for every contingency right down to assessing 6:00 a.m. as being the most likely time for everyone in the second floor flat to be asleep and therefore highly vulnerable. After the police chief explained every detail to the men involved, he added that because this arrest would take place in a middle-class residential area he wanted the officers to be careful not to use any offensive, foul language. One officer, speaking to the press, translated the order this way, "[You] might have to kill some son-of-a-bitch, but be a gentleman about it."[10]

Moments before the appointed hour, Sergeant Dolph Payne, followed by three other constables, their guns drawn, climbed the stairs to the Boyd's apartment. All the doors along the upstairs corridor stood closed. Kicking the first one open, Payne called out to his intended, "Boyd, it's Payne."[11] An empty room greeted the cop.

The group of lawmen proceeded to the second doorway. Again Payne called out to Boyd and identified himself. A single bed stood in the corner of this room. Payne did not bother to examine the bump under the pile of covers made by the sleeping Norman Boyd. As they kicked open the third and last door, Doreen Boyd sat up in bed.

"The police are here," she said simply.

No doubt confident that he was well beyond the hearing range of any language-sensitive citizen, Payne pounced on the sleeping form in the twin bed next to Dorreen's and instructed, "Not a goddamn move, Boyd, or I'll blow your head off."[12]

Neither sleepiness nor belligerent arrest procedures altered Boyd's extroverted personality.

"This is one way to meet you," he was reported as saying.[13]

Payne and the other arresting officers, however, showed considerably more interest in Boyd's bedside arsenal than his personality. A loaded .455 Smith and Wesson revolver, four other revolvers, and an unspecified number of automatic pistols lay within the sleeping man's reach. Police also confiscated more than $25,000 in cash from Edwin and Doreen's room in addition to a little over $1,500 cash from Norman's room. The younger Boyd protested long and loud that the cash was his savings and not spoils from a robbery. Unfortunately for Norman's financial well-being, the police found his claim somewhat suspect.

Moments later, Mayor Lamport, who also held the figurehead post of head of the police commission, joined the victorious officers at the scene. The normally sedate residential street turned into the venue for an impromptu, early morning party. As Lamport jumped excitedly up and down, reporters scurried madly about to get the story to their papers in time for the early edition.

Surrounded by publicity seekers and publicity mongers, Sergeant Dolph Payne quietly went about doing his job labelling and confiscating the objects found in the Boyds' suite. Among more mundane personal possessions, Payne found four hundred rounds of ammunition, knives, and an electric cattle prod.

Payne only entered into the frivolity when he'd completed the inventory. As he left the house, he picked up a stray cat which had wandered onto the front yard and, much to the delight of the press photographers gathered, he held the cat up and quipped, "This is our lucky cat. We take it with us on all our raids."14

The photographers made no effort to conserve film. Both the *Star* and the *Telegram* carried extra pages filled with every photograph that could conceivably be linked with the arrest. In addition to shots of Lamport and his daughters, there was an aerial shot of the neighbourhood where the arrest had occurred, pictures of both Leonard Jackson and Steve Suchan manacled to their beds in a Montreal hospital, and pictures of the bullet-proof vests worn by police during the raid. There were photos of all the detectives involved in the raid with each of the captives, pictures of Lamport with the detectives, and others with the mayor and the captives. There was even a picture of the pepper found in Boyd's pockets!

Reporters capitalized on the fact that when arrested Boyd had over $25,000 in his possession, while Leonard Jackson had been almost penniless. Pointing out this lack of financial equality, however, did little to shake the myth of "the Gang."

Sergeant of Detectives Edmund Tong died eight days after being advised that, at last, all the members of the Boyd Gang were now confined. For Tong it didn't matter that the security only proved to be temporary.

Boyd's new home was the antithesis of their "pleasant residential" hideaway: the maximum security wing of the Don Jail afforded very few amenities. Boyd spent his days contemplating a painless method of killing himself — he saw a successful suicide as a way to outsmart the authorities.

Usually an extrovert, Boyd taught himself to meditate. During his periods of meditation, images of escape gradually replaced thoughts of self-destruction. He found that by refusing to eat, which he'd been doing in an attempt to kill himself, his powers of concentration improved remarkably.

When authorities saw fit to transfer Willie Jackson from Kingston Penitentiary to the cell next to Boyd's, the move played directly into Boyd's new spiritual explorations.

Very much aware of the microphones hidden in their cells, the newly reunited pair discussed the world of religion endlessly and loudly. This only changed to a more private form of communication when Willie wisely proposed that Satan might be a more receptive audience than God.

Within a few days, the rebel angel saw fit to answer their prayers. Showing an amazing lack of forethought, authorities moved both Leonard Jackson and Steve Suchan from their hospital beds to the remaining two cells adjacent to Boyd's and Willie's. They had, at least, taken the precaution of confiscating Lennie's artificial foot.

Ever the jokester, Willie Jackson soon made friends with one of the guards assigned to their high-security corridor. As the guard led the four prisoners back to their cells after an exercise period, Willie grabbed the custodian's key and asked to be allowed to lock his friends in for the evening. The jailer, of course, denied Willie's request and demanded the key back. Willie obliged, assuring the guard he'd only been joking. The guard knew and enjoyed Willie's hijinks so the incident didn't cause the degree of concern that it certainly should have.

For the few seconds that Willie had held the key, he'd been squeezing it as tightly as he could in the palm of his hand. Once safely locked in his cell for the night, he used a jail-issue pencil to trace the outline imprinted in his hand.

Being such a likeable man, Willie had a great many friends. As he'd lived most of his life outside the law, his friends tended to be of the street-wise variety, and it didn't take too many visitors before Willie Jackson possessed a short, soft piece of metal and a file. All he and Boyd had to do was file the metal to match the pattern. To keep the guards from hearing the scraping of metal, they restricted their filing activity to coincide with the toilet flushing or when two or three of the gang were singing — passing the time, of course. The key, however, would only open one cell. They would need to saw through the bars of the other cells.

On his next visit, Willie's supplier brought them a hacksaw. The plan progressed well until one of the guards took to testing the window bars with a hammer. As it would take several days to saw right through the metal, this guard's overzealousness presented a formidable obstacle to the group's success. Neither Willie nor Boyd could think of a solution to the dilemma, so they used the system that had worked so well for them before: they prayed to Satan.

The next day the conscientious guard with the hammer booked off sick for a few days and the guard who had befriended Willie took his place. It was only a matter of time before they'd be free.

The authorities, of course, remained blissfully unaware of the group's plans. Lennie Jackson and Steve Suchan's trial for the murder of Sergeant of Detectives Edmund Tong was scheduled to begin at 9:00 a.m. on Monday, September 8, 1952. The gang got up very early that morning but not in preparation for any court appearances. They unlocked one cell door with their homemade key, pushed out the carefully filed bars and scaled the jails' walls. By the time guards noticed their disappearance, the four were enjoying the crisp autumn air, heading north through Toronto's natural system of ravines.

The *Telegram* advised Torontonians of the jailbreak with the headline, "BOYD, KILLER PALS LOOSE/POLICE [TO] 'SHOOT ON SIGHT'." The subhead quoted Doreen Boyd as saying her husband "Won't Be Taken Alive."[15] The opening words of the story reinforced the legend of the Boyd Gang for any who doubted it: an unnamed reporter began his retelling of the events with the words, "Edwin Boyd and Co."

Allan Lamport, who'd been so proud that morning in March when police captured Boyd felt this latest development was nothing short of shameful. A senior police officer described it as a disgrace.

The premier of Ontario ordered a full inquiry into security at the Don Jail. The guards, in the meantime, were relieved of their duties and replaced by members of the Ontario Provincial Police.

Advertisements from different agencies appeared in public places offering rewards totalling a previously-unheard-of $26,000. This amount would have purchased two more-than-adequate homes in Toronto at that time. Boyd became number one on Canada's "most wanted" list. A large picture of Doreen Boyd, with a copy of the previous day's *Telegram* in her left hand and a freshly lit cigarette in her right, declared, completely untruthfully, that she had no idea where her husband or his companions might be.

The newspapers also carried an open letter from Doreen to Ed asking him to please give himself up. She and her three children issued pleas on a local radio station, which included the children begging, "We miss you, Daddy, please come home." The excitement created by these dashing criminals swept across Canada. People loved to hate the Boyd Gang.

Concerned citizens reported numerous sightings of the gang members. Police followed up on each report. They took no chances on letting a lead slip through their fingers. The gang's family and friends were questioned repeatedly and kept under surveillance. A news release from the police chief's office assured Torontonians that police expected "a break soon."

The phrase must have been chosen more for its optimism than its accuracy because, unlike Boyd's capture six months earlier, the gang's final apprehension resulted from a coincidence and a citizen's report.

Tuesday, September 16, began the gang's second week of freedom. They hadn't gotten far, but apparently their choice of an abandoned farmstead to the north and east of the city was a judicious one because, so far, they hadn't been recaptured.

Lennie Jackson left his partners for awhile and returned with a replacement prosthesis strapped securely to the end of his left leg. Suchan also disappeared for a few hours and brought back fresh clothes for the group. Being able to get out of jail-issue denims they'd worn since the morning of their escape was an enormous relief, especially to Boyd and Suchan, who prided themselves on their appearance.

All four scavenged for fruit and vegetables from the adjacent farmers' fields. The bounty from these raids kept body and soul together, but barely. None of them had eaten any protein for more than a week. They were losing both strength and weight daily.

ONTARIO

ONTARIO PROVINCIAL POLICE

$26,000 Reward

EDWIN ALONZO BOYD. Alias Chas. B. HUNTER; alias Charles HUNTER; alias Jack THOMPSON; alias John HAWKINS, Age 37. 5'7½". Slim build. Black hair (grey). Blue eyes. Fresh comp.

WILLIAM RUSSELL JACKSON, alias A. GIBSON. Age 25. 5'7½". Medium build. Dk. br. hair. Blue eyes. Medium comp. "Eleanor" Tatooed right forearm.

LEONARD JACKSON, alias Robert KENT. Age 29. 5'9½". Medium build. Dk. br. Hair. Brown eyes. Dark Comp. Left foot artificial (limps).

VALENT LESSO alias Steve SUCHAN; alias Victor J. LENNOFF, Age 24. 5'10". Medium build. Brown hair. Brown eyes. Medium comp. Face pimply and pock-marked.

The GOVERNMENT OF THE PROVINCE OF ONTARIO will pay a reward of TWO THOUSAND DOLLARS for information resulting in the arrest of EACH of the above named persons who escaped from the Toronto Jail on the night of September 7th, 1952.

The BOARD OF COMMISSIONERS OF POLICE FOR THE CITY OF TORONTO will pay a reward of TWO THOUSAND DOLLARS for information resulting in the arrest of EACH of the above named persons. THIS REWARD IS IN ADDITION TO AND APART FROM the similar reward offered by the Province of Ontario.

In the event of more than one person claiming either, or both, of the above mentioned rewards or to be entitled to a share therein, the rewards will be apportioned as the ATTORNEY-GENERAL FOR ONTARIO deems just.

The CANADIAN BANKERS' ASSOCIATION, in addition to and apart from the rewards mentioned above, offers to pay a total reward of TEN THOUSAND DOLLARS for information resulting in the arrest of the persons named above.

The CANADIAN BANKERS' ASSOCIATION retains the unrestricted right to fix the amount to be paid in respect of each claim where more than one claim is made and to apply any part of the total reward in respect of each of the said persons arrested and the unrestricted right to reject any claim for reward. No claim for the BANKERS' ASSOCIATION REWARD will be considered unless made in writing to the Secretary of the Canadian Bankers' Association within thirty days after the date of the arrest in respect of which the reward is sought.

The CHIEF CONSTABLE OF TORONTO holds warrants for the arrest of VALENT LESSO alias STEVE SUCHAN and LEONARD JACKSON on charges of MURDER, ATTEMPTED MURDER and ROBBERY ARMED; and holds warrants for the arrest of WILLIAM RUSSELL JACKSON and EDWIN ALONZO BOYD on charges of ROBBERY ARMED.

ALL OF THESE MEN WILL NOW BE ARMED. THEY ARE EXTREMELY DANGEROUS AND THE UTMOST CARE SHOULD BE TAKEN IN EFFECTING THEIR ARREST.

Extradition proceedings will be instituted immediately in the event of these men being arrested in the United States or any foreign country. The identity of the person giving information will be kept strictly confidential.

Any person in possession of information regarding the whereabouts of these persons, or any one of them, should immediately communicate with the nearest police authority, the TORONTO CITY POLICE authorities or the undersigned.

Parliament Buildings,
Toronto, Ontario.
September 10th, 1952.

WILLIAM H. STRINGER
Commissioner of Police for Ontario.

(SEE FINGERPRINTS ON REVERSE SIDE)

The reward poster circulated throughout the country by the Ontario Provincial Police. At the time $26,000 was a substantial amount of money — more than enough to buy two very nice houses in the city of Toronto. (Courtesy of the Toronto Police Museum.)

Lennie suffered especially. The straw in the barn triggered his asthma and made breathing laboured. After eight days in these conditions, he was in very poor health.

Only Willie Jackson remained unaffected. His happy-go-lucky attitude, which had earned him the nickname "the clown," prevailed even under these circumstances. Hiding out, being captured and serving time were all part of the game for Willie.

The property where the gang holed up had been deserted for some time. Neighbouring farmers, brothers Bob and John Trimble, made a habit of checking the abandoned property periodically. The dramatic escape coupled with evidence of raids on their own gardens prompted them to make a more thorough investigation. In the house they found the remains of four straw mattresses. A search of the barn confirmed their suspicions. They'd heard reports of tramps in the area. They knew now where the drifters were staying. What they didn't know was whether or not their new neighbours were, in fact, the Boyd Gang — nor were they going to loiter long enough to find out. Bob and John Trimble returned to their own farm house and called the police.

Leads poured in faster than they could be followed up, so the Trimbles' call wasn't responded to until the next day. By then, an assortment of police departments had received reports, including one from workmen in the Trimbles' farm area who said they were talking to a man who'd emerged from the barn. He had appeared very pale, they explained, as though he'd been inside for a long time.

Others in the area spoke of their gardens being raided night after night, and of hearing dogs bark and shots being fired.

The wide-ranging search for the Boyd Gang narrowed to these few acres. They checked the farm house first and came up empty. With guns drawn, police made their way into the barn. The outlaws didn't have a chance. They sat perched in the rafters of their hideout. Their guns lay impotently on the floor below.

And so, after all the efforts by the Toronto police to capture Edwin Boyd, not once but now twice, two officers, this time from the North York police department, Detective Bert Trotter and Detective Sergeant Maurice Richardson made the final arrests.

Once outside the barn, now surrounded by other officers, all with their guns drawn, Boyd made a last attempt to talk his way out of an arrest. He told the officers his name was West and that he and his friends were merely in the barn to enjoy a libation together. He might as well have saved his breath: although all of the escaped convicts, especially Lennie, looked much worse than their photographs, their faces remained highly recognizable.

Handcuffed and at gun point, the arresting officers led the four to brand-new, state-of-the-art cells in the North York police station.

As it had in the early morning hours the previous March, a party-like atmosphere prevailed. Crowds gathered in North York as they had around the Don Jail. Everyone, it seemed, wanted at least a glimpse at the infamous Boyd Gang. Some were more fortunate than others.

Allan Lamport made an appearance at this capture as well and once again had his photograph taken with the captives. Much to the delight of the press, all but Lennie Jackson bantered back and forth promising to break out once again. Poor asthmatic Jackson was, by now, so sick that he likely viewed the arrest with relief. He needed medical attention quickly.

Police and government authorities wisely decided not to move the gang back to the cells they'd escaped from twice before until workers finished reinforcing the bars and changing the locks. When they were transferred back to the Don Jail, Boyd announced, much to the delight of the press, that he would break out again. The prophecy was merely an idle boast. Edwin Alonzo Boyd was not to be free again until authorities deemed he should be.

Lennie Jackson, somewhat recovered from the debilitating symptoms of his asthma, and Steve Suchan, the former violinist, were the first of the gang to be tried. The streets surrounding the Toronto City Hall courtroom became a circus of would-be spectators, armed police officers, and media.

Hastily assigned lawyers had little chance to reflect on the significance of their roles. The trials began less than a week after the capture. The group had escaped the day of Steve Suchan's and Lennie Jackson's scheduled trial for the murder of policeman Tong. Their disappearance had merely caused a postponement.

Two of Toronto's most respected criminal lawyers represented the convicts. Suchan's mother had once worked as a cleaner in the office building where John J. Robinette practiced law. One evening as she cleaned and the lawyer worked late, Suchan's mother hesitantly approached the man, explaining that her son was in trouble and asking Robinette to act as Steve's attorney. Because he liked the woman, he agreed to take on her son's case.

Lennie, however, was still without counsel the morning of his trial. At lunch hour that day, the judge, Chief Justice McRuer, happened to pass lawyer Arthur Maloney. The judge asked the younger man to represent Jackson in court. Although it wasn't a case he would have willingly taken on, Maloney accepted the challenge because he felt that not to do so would have offended the Chief Justice and that, of course, would not have been a wise career move.

There was little Robinette could do to protest his client's innocence. The dying Tong had positively identified Suchan as his assailant.

Maloney, however, argued that Lennie Jackson's most serious breech of ethics was that he was with Suchan when Tong had been killed. Neither the judge nor the jury bought this defense. The jury returned guilty verdicts on both prisoners, and McRuer sentenced both Lennie and Steve to be "hanged by the neck until you are dead." He scheduled the execution for December 16, 1952.

Suchan's parents each received nine-month jail terms for their parts in harbouring their son and his friends.

The charge against Doreen Boyd, harbouring a fugitive, was dismissed, possibly so that she might be with her three children. When authorities released Doreen she asked that the police return her personal effects. They granted the request unhesitatingly, and Doreen Boyd returned to her Pickering home a happy woman. She would not have to replace any of her toiletries. She had them all back now, including the box of tampons in which Edwin had cleverly hidden over $6,000.

After serving only three months in the Guelph Reformatory, Norman Boyd walked away a free man. Perhaps encouraged by his sister-in-law's success, he asked that the $1,500 police had confiscated be returned. It was.

Charges against Willie Jackson included breaking jail, escaping custody, and armed robbery. He received sentences totalling twenty years. When he heard this time would be served in the Kingston Penitentiary, "the clown" acted as though he'd been given a gift. He had many friends there, and his sentence would give him lots of time to visit with them.

Willie's brother, Joseph, wasn't quite as appreciative of the ten years the judge awarded him, nor was their brother-in-law, Allister Gibson, of his eight-year sentence. Both Joseph Jackson and Allister Gibson's terms resulted from the robbery of the bank at College and Manning branch on March 4, 1952. Boyd had led that attack.

Howard Gault, arrested fleeing the Dominion Bank he and Boyd had held up in October, 1951, was already cooling his heels in the Kingston Penitentiary. He had pleaded guilty to two armed robbery charges and was serving two concurrent seven-year terms.

Mary Mitchell, Lennie's sister and Suchan's girlfriend received a six-month sentence for harbouring Eddie Boyd and Willie Jackson.

Lennie and Steve's death penalties aside, Edwin Alonzo Boyd's sentence was the most severe. Charges against him included breaking jail, escaping custody twice, car theft, and eleven armed robberies. Both Ed and Doreen felt crushed as they listened to the judge announce a total of eight life sentences and an additional twenty-seven years.

And so justice finally broke apart the Boyd Gang. The legend, however, didn't die quite that easily. People talked about the dashing bank robbers, their reportedly luxurious lives and glamorous women for some time after. Eventually, though, the "gang" became old news, especially as many Canadians now enjoyed the wonder of television right in their own living rooms!

Leonard Jackson and Steve Suchan both died at the end of the hangman's rope on December 16, 1952, just as Chief Justice McRuer told them they would.

William Russell Jackson visited with his friends in the Kingston Penitentiary for fourteen years before being released in 1966.

Norman Boyd married, became a father, bought a home, and worked at a job that a sympathetic patron arranged for him.

Leonard Jackson's wife, Ann, remarried almost immediately. When that marriage broke up, the courts awarded custody of Lennie's son to her second husband. Ann's alcoholism was severe and the judge determined she was not capable of looking after the child. She died of cirrhosis of the liver.

Mary Mitchell entered the world's oldest profession and died prematurely of a brain tumor several years before Ann Jackson's death.

Anna Bosnich moved to the west coast where she pursued a successful career in real estate and raised Steve Suchan's child.

Suchan's parents served their time and then devoted the rest of their lives to their younger son.

Doreen and Eddie Boyd divorced. Doreen raised the three Boyd children. Both Doreen and Eddie remarried and, by coincidence, both chose to live the rest of their lives in British Columbia.

It took Eddie a little longer to get out west, though. After being paroled in 1962 he violated the conditions of his freedom by incurring unauthorized debts and indulging in a relationship with a sixteen-year-old girl. He was re-arrested. In November, 1965, he applied for parole again. Authorities deferred his request for a year.

Jack Webster, Historian for the Metropolitan Toronto Police, recently recalled, "As a rookie I walked the beat with Edwin Boyd's father. Years later I guarded him [Edwin] in city cells while he awaited trial. I told Boyd that his father had spoken frequently, and with great pride, of his son's Army service during the war. Boyd replied, 'He should still be proud of me. My picture's on the front page of the newspaper.'"[16]

Edwin Alonzo BOYD   #1728/51

1933, Nov. 20	Edmonton, Alta.	Vagrancy - Fined $20.00 & Costs or 6 weeks. as John Wilson Harkaway.
1935, Feb. 11	Saskatoon, Sask.	Vagrancy (Begging) - $3.00 Costs $1.75 or 2 months as John Gerald Adams.
1935, Nov. 27	USM St.Paul, Minn., USA	Violation of Immigration Laws - 24 hours in custody as Herbert John Hardley #2375.
1936, Aug. 10	Calgary, Alta.	Obtain Meal by Fraud - 3 days as Edwin Boyd #9890.
193-, Sept. 3	Edmonton, Alta.	1. Break, enter & theft (16 charges) - 3½ years concurrent 2. Break & enter with intent (2 charges) - 3½ years concurrent. 3. Break & enter - 3½ years concurrent. 4. Theft - 6 months concurrent as Edwain Boyd. #3044.
1939, Mar. 15		Released on Ticket-of-Leave. Sentence due to Expire August 15th, 1939.
1951, Oct. 17		Arrested on a charge of Bank Robbery. While on remand till November 7th, 1951 and in custody of Toronto Mail he escaped on Sunday November 4th, 1951.
1952, Mar. 15		Re-arrested in Toronto. In custody Toronto Jail charged with Armed Robbery of Several Banks. Escaped from Toronto Jail morning of 8th September 1952.
1952. Sept. 16.		Re-captured.
1952. Oct. 16.	Toronto Ont.	1st Charge:- Rob while armed . Bank of Montreal 2015 Avenue Rd on 9th Sept/49. of $2256. 2nd Charge:- Rob while armed. Bank of Commerce. 788 O'Connor Drive. on 18th Jan/50. of $2862. 3rd Charge:- Rob while armed. Dominion Bank. Dufferin & Glencairn Ave on 4th July/50. of $1954. 4th Charge:- Rob while armed. Bank of Montreal 2015 Avenue Rd on 19th March/51 of $3021. 5th Charge:- Rob while armed. Dominion Bank. 187 Shepherd Ave on 1st Sept/51. of $8029. 6th Charge:- Rob while armed. Dominion Bank. Lawrence & Yonge on 16th Oct/51. of $12,234 7th Charge:- Rob while armed. Royal Bank. Leaside Ont. on 30th Nov/51. of $46,207 8th Charge:- Rob while armed. Bank of Montreal, College & Manning Ave on 4th March/52 of $24,696 9th Charge:- Assault with intent to rob W.H.Gibson Smith and William Boyce of Imperial Bank Fairlawn & Avenue Rd on 11th Oct/50. (Armed with an Offensive Weapon.) 10th Charge:- Theft of auto from Wilson Turner. 11th Charge:- Theft of auto from William C. Keast. 12th Charge:- Break Jail on 4th Nov/51 (Toronto Jail.) 13th Charge:- Escape from Toronto Jail. on 4th Nov/51. 14th Charge:- Escape from Toronto Jail. on 8th Sept/52. Committed to Kingston Pen'y for LIFE on charges 1 to 8 incl: 10 years on 9th charge, 4 years on 10th charge, 4 years on 11t charge, 5 years on 12th charge, 2 years on 13th charge, & 2 y on 14th charge. by Judge Forsyth. (The 2 years on each of charges 13 & 14. are to run consecutively.)

Edwin Alonzo Boyd's original "rap" sheet headed up with his name and convict number. Note the uneven darkness of the print so characteristic of a manual typewriter. (Courtesy of the Toronto Police Museum.)

THE BOYD GANG'S BANK ROBBERIES

1. Bank of Montreal, Armour Heights Branch, Avenue Road, September 9, 1949. Take — $2,200. Edwin Boyd, alone.
2. Canadian Bank of Commerce, St. Clair and O'Connor, January 18, 1950. Take — $2,8862. Edwin Boyd, alone.
3. Dominion Bank, Dufferin and Glencairn, July 31, 1950. Take — $1,954. Edwin Boyd and Howard Gault.
4. Imperial Bank of Canada, Avenue Road and Fairlawn, October 11, 1950. Take — $0.00. Edwin Boyd, alone.
5. Bank of Montreal, Armour Heights Branch, Avenue Road, March 19, 1951. Take — police reported $6,000; Boyd maintained the amount was $2,900. Edwin Boyd, alone.
6. Dominion Bank, Lansing Branch, Sheppard Avenue, September 1, 1951. Take — $8,029.70. Edwin Boyd, Howard Gault and possibly Norman Boyd (Ed's younger brother).
7. Dominion Bank, Lawrence and Yonge Street, October 16, 1951. Take — $12,234, total amount recovered by police within minutes. Edwin Boyd and Howard Gault.
8. Bank of Toronto, Dundas and Roncesvalles, November 20, 1951. Take — $4,300. Edwin Boyd, Steve Suchan, Willie Jackson, Lennie Jackson (no relation to one another) and possibly Norman Boyd.
9. Royal Bank, Leaside Branch, November 30, 1951. Take — $46,207.13. Edwin Boyd, Steve Suchan, Willie Jackson and Lennie Jackson.
10. Bank of Toronto, Kingston Road Branch, January 25, 1952. Take — $10,400. Edwin Boyd, Steve Suchan and Joseph Jackson (Willie Jackson's brother).
11. Bank of Montreal, College and Manning Branch, March 4, 1952. Take — $24,696. Edwin Boyd, Joseph Jackson and his brother-in-law, Allister Gibson.

All bank addresses given are in Toronto.
Police records and other sources are inconsistent in their lists of some of the participants in some of the robberies.

NOTES

SIEGE AT OAK LAKE

Except where noted, all references are to the *Winnipeg Free Press*, 1978 editions.

<table>
<tbody>
<tr><td>1 - 2</td><td>23 January.</td></tr>
<tr><td>3</td><td>24 November.</td></tr>
<tr><td>4</td><td>28 November.</td></tr>
<tr><td>5 - 8</td><td>24 January.</td></tr>
<tr><td>9 - 10</td><td>23 January.</td></tr>
<tr><td>11</td><td>The Stockholm Syndrome is an identifiable psychological phenomenon: the positive bonding that can occur during a kidnapping or hostage taking. The condition is named after the city in Sweden where an incident took place, 10 September 1973, in which bank robbers took customers hostage, and the hostages began to side with their captors — to the extent that one female customer/hostage engaged in sexual relations with one of the robbers.</td></tr>
<tr><td>12</td><td>23 January.</td></tr>
<tr><td>13</td><td>24 January.</td></tr>
<tr><td>14</td><td>30 January.</td></tr>
<tr><td>15</td><td>*Calgary Herald*, 27 January 1978.</td></tr>
<tr><td>16 - 17</td><td>27 January.</td></tr>
<tr><td>18 - 19</td><td>30 January.</td></tr>
<tr><td>20</td><td>28 January.</td></tr>
<tr><td>21</td><td>26 January.</td></tr>
<tr><td>22</td><td>27 January. (The newspaper erroneously gave Hornseth's rank as Constable.)</td></tr>
<tr><td>23 - 24</td><td>27 January.</td></tr>
<tr><td>25 - 26</td><td>28 January.</td></tr>
<tr><td>27 - 37</td><td>30 January.</td></tr>
<tr><td>38</td><td>6 December.</td></tr>
<tr><td>39 - 40</td><td>21 November.</td></tr>
<tr><td>41 - 42</td><td>24 November.</td></tr>
<tr><td>43</td><td>25 November.</td></tr>
<tr><td>44</td><td>1 December.</td></tr>
<tr><td>45 - 49</td><td>30 November.</td></tr>
<tr><td>50 - 53</td><td>7 December.</td></tr>
<tr><td>54 - 57</td><td>8 December.</td></tr>
<tr><td>58 - 61</td><td>9 December.</td></tr>
<tr><td>62 - 66</td><td>11 December.</td></tr>
<tr><td>67</td><td>5 January 1979.</td></tr>
<tr><td>68 - 69</td><td>17 January 1979.</td></tr>
</tbody>
</table>

NO FOOL LIKE AN OLD FOOL

All references are to the *Halifax Herald*, 1922 editions.

1 - 2   30 August.
3   The spellings of the following names are inconsistently recorded: Grey/Gray, MacKay/McKay, McMellon/McMillan, Simms/Sims. Spellings used in this retelling have been chosen because they were used more frequently throughout the reports.
4 - 9   30 August.
10 - 11   31 August.
12 - 18   6 September.
19 - 24   7 September.
25 - 26   24 November.

SUMMER OF CARNAGE

Information for this story was compiled from articles appearing in the following newspapers: Vancouver *Province*, 29, 30, and 31 August 1982; 14, 15, 16, 20, 21, and 24 September 1982; 16 February 1983; 19 May 1983; 19 October 1983; *Vancouver Sun*, 9, 14, 15, 16, and 22 September 1982; 10 January 1986; *Globe and Mail*, 16 September 1982; *Calgary Herald*, 19 and 21 October 1983; 15, 17, and 18 April 1984; 10 January 1986; *Toronto Star*, 28 August 1983; 20, 21, and 30 October 1983; 22 November 1983; 16, 17, and 18 April 1984; *Winnipeg Free Press*, 13 September 1983; and the Kamloops *News*, 16 April 1984.

1   *Toronto Star*, 20 October 1983.
2   Telephone conversation with Flathead County Sheriff's office, June 9, 1994.

THE DEADLY DOCTOR

Information for this story was compiled from articles appearing in the Montreal *Gazette*, 6 and 7 December 1935, 22 May 1952, and 12 June 1953, as well as from extensive research data kindly supplied by author Frank Anderson, Gopher Books, Saskatoon, Saskatchewan.

ALL IN THE FAMILY

1   *The Last Dance: Murder in Canada*, by Neil Boyd, Prentice-Hall Canada, Scarborough, Ontario, 1988.
2   *The Robert Cook Murder Case*, by Frank Anderson, Gopher Books, Saskatoon, Saskatchewan, 1978.
3 - 4   *Edmonton Sun*, 26 February 1984.
5   *Edmonton Sun*, 29 February 1984.

THE FAT LADY SINGS

Except where noted, all references are to the Montreal *Gazette*, 1949 editions.

1	10 September.
2	26 September.
3	10 September.
4 - 6	24 September.
7 - 9	26 September.
10	27 September.
11	30 September.
12 - 17	15 March 1950.
18	14 December 1950.
19	12 January 1951.

WHEN TORONTO-THE-GOOD WENT BAD

1	*The Boyd Gang,* by Marjorie Lamb and Barry Pearson, Peter Martin and Associates, Toronto, 1976.
2	*The Boyd Gang.*
3	*Toronto Telegram,* 7 March 1952.
4	*The Boyd Gang.*
5	Toronto Telegram, 21 (?) November 1951.
6	*The Boyd Gang.*
7	*Toronto Telegram,* 6 (?) March 1952.
8	*The Boyd Gang.*
9	*Toronto Telegram,* 13 (?) March 1952.
10 - 14	*The Boyd Gang.*
15	*Toronto Telegram,* 8 (?) September 1952.
16	Telephone conversation with Jack Webster, February 1994.